D0856720

Let's Ride!

WITH LINDA TELLINGTON-JONES

Linda Tellington-Jones
Andrea Pabel • Hilmar Pabel

Let's Ride!

WITH LINDA TELLINGTON-JONES

Fun and TTeamwork with your Horse or Pony

Trafalgar Square Publishing

Publishers call this the copyright page. It tells you who has made this book: the authors, photographers, illustrators, men and women at the publishing companies, and the printers.

First published in the United States of America in 1997 by Trafalgar Square Publishing, North Pomfret, Vermont 05053

Printed by Dah Hua Printing Press Co. Ltd, Hong Kong

© English language edition Trafalgar Square Publishing, USA and Kenilworth Press Ltd, UK, 1997.

English language edition published simultaneously in Great Britain by Kenilworth Press Ltd and in the United States of America by Trafalgar Square Publishing in 1997.

First published in Germany under the title *Die Linda Tellington-Jones Reitschule* by Franckh-Kosmos Verlags-GmbH & Co, Stuttgart, in 1996.

All rights reserved. No part of this publication may be reproduced, stored in a retrieval system, or transmitted in any form or by any means, electronic, mechanical, photocopying, recording or otherwise, without the prior permission of the copyright holders.

ISBN 1-57076-085-3

Library of Congress Catalog Card Number: 96-60007

The black and white drawings in the boxes and the "At a glance" sections were drawn by Marianne Golte-Bechtle, who also did the black and white drawings on pages 19, 28, 41, 45, 48, 49, 50, 51, 54 and 90. The illustration on page 17 is by Rahel Schale. All other illustrations are from Linda Tellington-Jones.

"Angie", the Guardian Angel of Horses, was drawn by Gisela Dürr and the cover design was by Paul Saunders using color photos by Hilmar Pabel.

Hilmar Pabel, Rimsting, Germany, has taken almost all of the color photos in this book. Eight other photos have been used: Maria Verdiccio, Vancouver, Canada, page 7 (middle left); Edgar Schöpal, Düsseldorf, Germany, page 13 (bottom); Sarah Fisher, Bath, England, page 32; Andrea Pabel, Taos, New Mexico, USA, page 67 (top and middle), page 104 (middle and bottom). The two color photos on page 13 (middle) and all the black and white photos on the pages 10-12 are from Linda Tellington-Jones' personal photo album.

A note from Linda

For the sake of brevity in this book I have chosen to refer to each of the humans as "she", and to all of the horses as "he" unless, of course, I'm talking about someone of a specific gender.

Disclaimer of Liability:
The Authors and Publisher shall have neither liability nor responsibility to any person or entity with respect to any loss or damage caused or alleged to be caused directly or indirectly by the information contained in this book. While the book is as accurate as the Authors can make it, there may be errors, omissions and inaccuracies.

This book is dedicated with love to my entire family. To my parents, Marion and Harold Hood, my sisters Robyn Hood and Susan Hodgson, and my brothers Gerry, John and Randy.

Contents

Linda's Tip

In this book you'll find lots of information and many new ideas. Woven thoughout the book are stories about my experiences with horses. Added to this are tips, ideas, Angie's opinions and many photos and illustrations to make it easy for you to understand.

• Don't be discouraged if some things seem complicated in the written description. Take time to look at the step-by-step photos and try to visualize as much as possible before practicing. You might try it on a friend for feedback.

If you want more information about TTEAM there are regular clinics, many books and videos, a newsletter, and a list of practitioners available from the TTEAM offices. You can also order the special TTEAM tools and equipment (see page 116).

• If you want to find a certain subject quickly in this book you can look it up in the index on page 119.

My name is Allison. I am eleven years old and my favorite horse is an Icelandic, Frissi. I started to ride five years ago.

Angie says

I'm Angie, the Guardian Angel of Horses. Horses are misunderstood and treated poorly too often. It's my wish that you will always be friendly and fair to your horse. In this book I speak for the horses, so you'll be able to understand them better. Then they'll really be your friends and they can teach you so much!

My name is Amadeus and I am five years old.

My name is Shanti. I am nine years old and started to ride three years ago. My pony, Pepper, is my best friend.

My name is Claire. I am ten years old and have two favorite horses at home: Jed and an Appaloosa mare, Demi.

My name is Talia. I am thirteen years old and have been riding for two years. My horse, Oliver, is a Thoroughbred-cross.

My name is Mandy. I am thirteen years old. My horse, Borkur, is twice my age and taught me to ride.

My name is Geoff. I am thirteen years old and have not been riding very long. I really have fun with horses and like them a lot.

At a glance

What is TTEAM℠?

TTEAM stands for "Tellington-Jones Equine Awareness Method". The method uses bodywork and ground exercises to help train horses to be safe and cooperative partners, improve their performance, and develop a deeper friendship with them.

The TTEAM℠ method concentrates on three areas:

- TTouch℠ bodywork – a system of specific touches over the entire body of the horse.
- Confidence Course – leading exercises in various positions and working with horses in hand over many different obstacles.
- Riding with awareness, fun and a balanced seat – a combination I call "The Joy of Riding".

The letters ℠ behind the words TTEAM and TTouch means that these words are registered.

I want to thank you

This book is the result of the close cooperation of many people who became like family during the week of teaching and photographing the children for this book.

First, I'd like to express my heartfelt thanks and my great admiration for our photographer Hilmar Pabel, who at age eighty-five amazed and impressed all of us. The energy and stamina he showed while taking more than 2000 photographs during my clinic in Canada, inspired and encouraged us again and again.

Many thanks also to Hilmar's wife Romy, who was with us in Canada. I have enjoyed her patience and good humor as well as her wonderful hospitality in the Pabel home, on the Chiemsee in Germany.

It was at Chiemsee that I worked on the final draft of this book with my co-author, Andrea Pabel, who presents my work with children with such charm and skill. In the early eighties, twenty-year-old Andrea participated in my training program and became a TTEAM practitioner. I never dreamed that one day we would write a book together. Andrea's life-long experience with horses, her many years of practicing the TTEAM work, and her training as a Feldenkrais practitioner, combined with her talent and experience as a writer of children's books, have brought this book to fruition.

My warmest thanks also to:

• My sister Robyn and my brother-in-law Phil, who hosted our TTEAM clinic on their Icelandic breeding farm. Robyn has made major contributions to the development of the TTEAM work over the past twenty years.

• Christine Schwartz, Robyn's right-hand assistant, who prepared such delicious lunches for us, and Christine's mother, Frau Schwartz, who encouraged our group continuously;

• Sheila Goertz of Asmura Arabians;

• Stefan and Andrea Bundschuh, the directors of "Fohlenhof", and its owner Michael Davies;

• Hilda and Ron Wohlford of the Aspengrove Equestrian Training Center who so kindly allowed us to use their school horses and equestrian facilities;

• Emmy Kennedy, our humorous hostess at the Falcon Nest bed and breakfast;

• Sandra Wilson, who accompanied Shanti and Claire and got along so wonderfully with Amadeus;

• Maria Verdiccio who so conscientiously helped with the horses and jumped in wherever help was needed;

• Erika Müller, long-standing editor-in-chief of the German horse magazine *Freizeit im Sattel* for her helpful advice in the planning stages of this book;

• Kate Prentice and her mother Delphine for their warm hospitality and care at their country house near London, where we met to select the photographs;

• Kirsten Henry, who assisted me with the editing of the first galleys in Santa Fe with great precision, dedication and enthusiasm;

• Hans Schindler for his deep understanding of my work and sensitive afterword to this book.

All the children and helpers got together for this photo. We are doing some Ear Touches to relax. You see, it's not just for horses!

I invited five girls and two boys for a week-long riding clinic to Vernon, Canada, in the summer of 1995. I would like to thank each one for their contribution:

• My niece Mandy, who had just returned from a very demanding training session in

Linda's Tip

Throughout my life I have ridden many different horses. In this book you will also be introduced to lots of breeds. We can learn something from all of them and it is this variety that makes riding fun and helps us to gain experience and knowledge.
• The children in this course have asked question after question. They wanted to know why I do some things in ways other than they have learned in their riding schools at home. Maybe you will ask the same questions as you read through the book. I would like you to think about what you do with your horses and how you treat them. Develop your intuition about what to do. There are many different methods of riding and training horses. Many will tell you horses must be punished to obey you. I like to use the golden rule. Treat your horse as you would like to be treated. Using TTEAM techniques you can be kind, fair and successful and develop a special relationship with your horse.

Talking with my co-author, Andrea Pabel.

With my sister and closest co-worker, Robyn Hood.

Our photographer, Hilmar Pabel – in action from early morning until dusk.

Hilmar Pabel has brought us the first photos. We get to pick!

uxembourg for junior riders but vas fully present and enthusiastic n spite of jetlag.

• The siblings Geoff and llison, who were tireless and lways in a good mood.

• Claire and Shanti whom I ave known since they were born. Vhen she was three years old, I ut Shanti on her first horse. Vhen Claire could barely walk I ook her in a backpack in the orests to search for the fairies.

• Talia, whose mother Leora aster and grandmother Mia egal are like family to me. It's een wonderful to watch Talia's ove of horses and riding skills levelop over the years.

• Amadeus, Andrea Pabel's son and Romy and Hilmar Pabel's grandson. It was a pleasure to see his courage and athletic ability on horseback at only five years old.

I also would like to thank everyone at Franckh-Kosmos publishing house who had a hand in making this book possible. And to my German editor Almuth Sieben, who invested so much time and love into the planning and realization of this book.

My very special thanks and appreciation to my American publisher, Caroline Robbins, for the remarkable attention to detail and brilliant editing of this book into English. It was a pleasure and inspiration to work with her. And my great appreciation to my British publishers, David and Dee Blunt, and Lesley Gowers of Kenilworth Press for their skillful input and enthusiastic support and for being such lovely folks.

Finally my great thanks to all the horses without whom this book would not exist. I encourage you to open your heart, to see horses with new eyes and to honor them as our teachers. Remember the golden rule and treat your horse as you would like to be treated.

A life for horses

"Early practice!" At eleven months old in my aunt's lap I am trying out the Ear TTouch with a bear cub.

With my little sister, Susan, on my second horse, "Beauty".

It doesn't always have to be a horse! My bull calf, Dale, liked being ridden too.

I had the good fortune to grow up in a big family with two sisters and three brothers on a farm near Edmonton, Alberta, Canada. Animals, especially horses, were an important part of our lives.

When I was six years old and started going to school my father gave me my first horse. There was a very practical reason for this: in those days there were no school buses in rural Canada and Trixie was my only "means of transportation" to and from school. I had to ride about five miles every day, rain or shine.

Trixie was not an easy horse. She had a very strong-willed personality. When I first rode her in an arena I couldn't keep her from running away with me back to her stall. To this day it's a mystery why my father bought her for me! Maybe she was the only horse for sale. Later, I fell off many times when she took off and headed back to the barn. Once I got so angry that I pinned clothespins on her ears as a punishment... my first try at ear work. Unfortunately, it didn't help in Trixie's case!

When I was eleven years old I started training every day at Briarcrest Stables, a well-known training center for hunters and jumpers. Under the skilled tutelage of owner and trainer Alice Metheral I started many horses under saddle and was soon competing successfully in horse shows. Every day I rode three to four horses after school. I think the experience of riding so many different horses, combined with my special relationship with them is the secret of my success.

First success

When I was fourteen I began to teach riding classes at Briarcrest Stables. At that time I had a wonderful mare named Angel who really deserved her name. I could ride her home from the pasture bareback with nothing on her head. We both enjoyed it so much that we sometimes practiced bridleless in the arena and progressed to the point of jumping an entire course bareback. I'll never forget that blissful feeling of flying over the jumps with Angel.

I participated annually in the famous nine-day Edmonton Spring Horse Show. When I was fifteen the rider of one of Alberta's top jumpers broke his arm and asked me to show his horse, named Bouncing Buster, for him. Bouncing Buster was a small Quarter Horse, only 14.2 hands with a big jump in him. Although I had never ridden the horse before and had only ten minutes to warm him up for the first go-round, we qualified for the finals and won the competition with jumps over five feet. My experiences riding so many different horses paid off and, of course, Bouncing Buster was simply a fantastic jumper!

Some years later I married and moved with my husband, Wentworth Tellington, to California. Went had received his riding training in the American cavalry and was an expert horseman. We spent four years at a boarding school as teachers, where I taught social studies and riding and cared for the horses. At that time I had my first experiences ith therapeutic riding. I taught a velve-year-old-girl who was deaf nd dumb to ride. Not only did ne learn to ride, but she took part junior jumping classes.

Later on, I developed a three-nonth training program for enagers who were mentally hallenged. Riding without a addle gave them a feeling of ndependence and strengthened neir self-confidence. I also taught ding in the US Pony Club, an rganization which teaches all vels of horsemanship to riders etween the ages of six and ghteen. Many Olympic riders arted as Pony Clubbers.

1960 my husband and I ounded the Hemet Breeding arm in southern California. We ad eighty Thoroughbred brood nares, four breeding stallions and venty Arabian broodmares on ur farm. In 1961 we organized ne first of many years of summer amps for junior riders between ne ages of nine and eighteen. We taught the kids to trust their orses and to be confident in the addle – basic requirements for n riding. And more than that, e taught horsemanship and nything to do with horses. eeding, unsoundnesses, bridling, addling, grooming, breed cognition, were all part of the rogram. Fun was a main gredient of our summer camps: e jumped without saddles, with ands stretched out to the side, ent swimming with our horses nd played many riding games.

1964 we founded the Pacific oast Equestrian Research Farm nd School of Horsemanship, a onderful school offering clinical udies of horses and a nine-nonth residential training rogram for riding instructors. fter ten years, I began to feel that there was something more important than turning out prize-winning riding instructors. I felt that I needed to communicate to people the important role animals play in our lives and how much they have to teach us. I closed the school, sold sixty horses to good homes and headed off for a two-year trip around the world. I had been teaching for twenty-three years. It was time for me to learn and to find a new challenge.

New paths

I used to imagine having little antennas on my head, like an ant. When I didn't know what to do I'd use my antennas to check out a new direction. When something doesn't feel right, I won't do it. But when my antennae say yes, I go forward. My antennae led me to Germany in 1975, where I met Ursula Bruns, the editor of a German horse magazine, and was invited to train four horses and three other riders for Equitana, an international exhibition in Essen, Germany. During my stay in Germany I worked with many horses and riders and spent three months teaching therapeutic riding and learning German at the Jugendfarm, owned by the Boehm family in Stuttgart. It's a farm where children can come every afternoon to play, take care of the animals and learn to ride.

In 1975 I began professional training in the Feldenkrais Method. This method teaches humans to move and use their bodies in new ways through gentle, non-habitual movements. Feldenkrais can greatly improve athletic performance, and it is wonderful for healing injuries. At first I thought I would use the Feldenkrais Method to train

Two who really got along: with "Blaze" in the pasture.

Fifteen years old at the Edmonton Spring Horse Show.

In 1953 the "Riding Hoods" are winning the "Family Ride" class at the Edmonton Horse Show.

Conditioning Bint Gulida in the sand dunes by Del Mar, California in 1961. Four weeks earlier we had won a 100-mile endurance race.

Bint Gulida and me two weeks after she set her endurance record.

Point to point: competition at the Pebble Beach hunter trials in 1973.

riding instructors. But suddenly a thought hit like lightning: if this method works so well for humans, won't it work just as well for horses? They have a nervous system, a skeleton and patterns of movements, just like us. I couldn't let go of this thought and could hardly wait to try it out.

In the first week of the training I worked with a friend's mare using the Feldenkrais Method and was amazed at the results. I began to see horses with new eyes. A big "Ah-ha" came when I first realized that horses who are thought to be "mean" – who buck, kick, bite or pin their ears back – almost always have a reason. They can be fearful because of past bad experiences which make them tense, or they are sore and not feeling well. This was the beginning of a new understanding of horses and led to the development of the TTEAM work.

At first I found many ways of using ground exercises like the Labyrinth, plastic and the Star to teach horses to cooperate without force and learn how to learn. It was eight years later when I discovered the TTouch and a whole new system evolved.

In 1992 I was awarded the "Lifetime Achievement Award for Outstanding Contribution to the Art and Science of Riding" from the American Riding Instructors Association. This award is given very rarely and I am very honored and proud of it. A year later, to my great surprise and joy, the North American Horse Association named me "Horsewoman of the Year 1993".

Help for "Free Willy"

I not only work with horses but with many different animals: monkeys, snakes, rabbits, guinea pigs, bears, cats and dogs. I have been able to help many animals like iguanas, birds and tigers in the big zoos around the world with the TTouches. Perhaps you've heard of the orca whale who starred in the movie "Free Willy"? His living situation – in too small a tank – was very damaging and stressful. He needed help, but was afraid of the veterinarians who wanted to treat him. After I worked on him with the TTouch, he became more trusting.

"How can you work with so many different animals?" I'm often asked. I completely tune into the animal until there is no separation between us. After a while, I feel as if we are one. If you really think about it, humans and animals have a lot more in common than we know.

I've noticed that children often communicate with animals naturally. Unfortunately many adults lose that connection when they grow up. With the TTouch you can regain this connection and have a deeper relationship with the animal kingdom. Children who are afraid of animals or who don't feel a strong connection can use TTEAM work to make friends with them.

Many children have the patience to spend hours with a horse, caressing and talking to him. Childrens' love for horses is so natural and unspoiled that horses will do things for them they would never do for adults. That's why I wrote this book for you, horse-loving children and teenagers. But grown ups will also find a lot that is new and interesting. Show this book to adults and discuss it with them.

My hope is that you never lose your connection with your horse. I'd like to show you how to naintain friendship and magic in hat relationship. You and your orse or pony will be happier and nore successful, whether you ride for fun or are actively showing and competing.

Some years ago I wrote a poem that I want to share with you.

The "Riding Hoods" on my Dad's eightieth birthday in 1989.

Angel Guardians of the Animals

Fairies care for nature
Yes?
But how about animals
Must I guess?
Or need I only ask
Are animals also
A fairy task?

The answer comes back
Loud and clear
The angels care
For animals dear

The animal spirits
Gather 'round
Their loving protection
Does abound

Each species has
An angel guide
Close to protect them
At their side

If you open your heart
You'll see them there
Soften your eyes
You cannot stare
Their loving presence
Fills the air

As you reach out
and caress an animal
friend, you also, will
be touched by the presence
of angelic gentleness and
filled with the spirit of light

Protected closely
In the night
The feathered softness
Of etheric wings
Brings sweet melody
When an angel sings

So open your ears
To celebrate songs
You may even hear
Chanting
And sacred gongs

Still your breath
To feel movement of air
When you sit
With your horse
Or your dog
Or your hare
Always remember
The angels are there.

A sensitive giant. The orca whale who starred in "Free Willy" enjoys the TTouch all over.

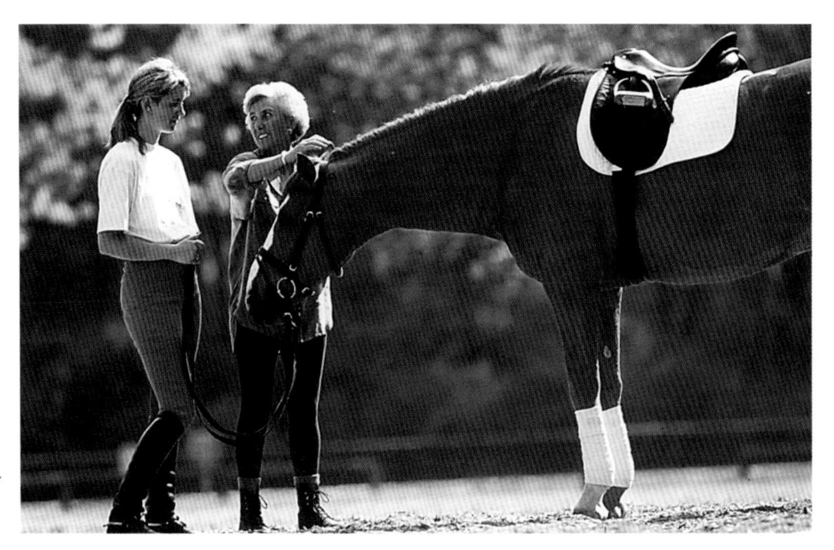
"He keeps getting better". Short conference with German Olympic rider Nicole Uphoff-Becker and "Daydream".

With the Icelandics

On a beautiful August morning we all meet at the farm owned by my sister Robyn Hood and my brother-in-law Phil Pretty. They breed Icelandic horses in the green hills of Vernon, British Columbia, Canada. Their daughter Mandy has had the good fortune to have been raised here, and it goes without saying, she knows Icelandics very well. Her friends and next-door neighbors, Allison and Geoff, are at the farm almost every day, so they know the horses well, too. The other children have never met an Icelandic before!

First, I suggest a walk around the pastures, so we can get to know the horses.

"I thought we were going to ride right away!" says Claire.

"A little later." I say, "First, let's just observe the horses. It's really interesting! Sometimes it makes me feel like a detective."

"The more we know about a horse, the better we can understand him and learn to treat him well."

We arrive in a big pasture with mares and foals. A stallion is grazing peacefully with them.

"Now take a good look: how do the horses relate to one another? Which horses chase others away? Who comes to greet you? Which horses keep their distance, or seem timid or even suspicious?"

Shanti calls: "There are two foals playing!"

They nip at each other's necks, rear and gallop off, obviously friends.

A mouse-gray mare comes slowly closer to greet us, but some of the other horses don't seem to be very interested in our visit.

Angie says

Have you been told that horses have no feelings? I knew a horse who didn't eat for days because his companion horse had been taken away. Every horse can feel sadness and anger, joy and pain, can be timid or brave. Take the time to observe how your horse is expressing his feelings. Then you will be able to understand him even better.

After a walk around the pasture we catch four calm horses to take a closer look at them.

"What do you see?" I ask. We begin to collect impressions. We compare their conformation and also the form and placement of their ears and nostrils. Then we come closer and look for swirls under their thick forelocks. Horses are all different; the shape of their heads, eyes and ears are unique. From these physical characteristics, I can learn something about their personalities. My grandfather, Will Caywood, who was named "Trainer of the Year" at the Moscow Hippodrome in Russia in 1905, whilst training racehorses for Czar Nicholas II, also taught me to read the meaning of a horse's facial swirls.

Later I studied the personality of horses all over the world, led a research project on the subject and wrote a book.

Here are a few guidelines to the art of interpreting the personalities of horses. Horses whose ears are wider apart at the top than at the base are likely to have a reliable temperament. Horses with a heart-shaped uppe

A gray mare approaches our group with interest.

She enjoys the Mouth TTouch.

p are often very curious and
eem to enjoy contact with
umans. A flat, soft chin shows
hat a horse is very intelligent; he
night untie knots and learn to
pen gates, which can sometimes
e a nuisance.

Naturally, when you're
valuating a horse's personality
om his features you must also
ake into consideration the way he
being stabled, fed, treated and
dden.

"It's very rewarding, getting to
now your horse well," I explain
the children. "You can develop
special partnership from better
nderstanding."

"Of course!" calls Shanti. "My
ony Pepper is my friend. If we

Linda's Tip

Observing horses

Take the time to watch a horse in a field or a corral. You can focus on the following things and even take notes:

- Does the horse move a lot or a very little? Does he rest frequently?
- Is he nervous and restless or is he really able to relax?
- Does he run and play with the other horses?
- What is his head carriage like? Does he carry his head high all the time, or does he lower it and relax?
- Which horses does he like or dislike?
- How does he react to unusual noises?

I am sure you will notice even more. When you know your horse well, you'll be able to understand him and be his friend.

ne Icelandic foal curiously peeks out from behind her mother.

idn't have such a good
elationship, we wouldn't be so
uccessful in competitions.
here's a lot he does just for me."

"There's a lot you do just for him. You make sure you have time for him, and when you do the TTouch and groundwork with him, you'll make your connection even deeper. For me, this is all a part of riding. Riding is only one aspect of the relationship we have with our horses. Mutual respect, trust and friendship goes beyond good riding. That's what I call real 'horsemanship'. It makes a huge difference whether you force a horse to obey, or if he follows your aids willingly because you've won his trust."

Geoff shows me two photos he brought with him and asks:

"What do you think of him? That's Coke, he belongs to a friend of mine. He has a reputation for being difficult."

I examine the pictures closely, then hold them so that everyone can see.

"What do you think?"

"He has small eyes," says Allison.

"The upper lip is longer than the lower lip," remarks Claire.

"And what does that mean?" Talia wonders.

"The small, half-closed eye tells me that Coke is an introverted horse. That's why he reacts slowly. The longer, upper lip means that a horse has a tendency

This horse has small jowls, a sign of limited intelligence. His owners tell us that he has difficulty understanding the rider's signals and is not very cooperative.

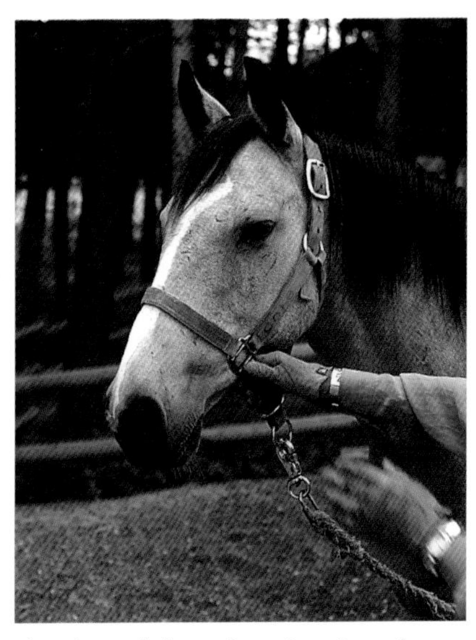

The almond-shaped eye is a sign of a introverted, strong-willed horse. The slight moose nose below the halter shows his strong personality.

to be insecure. He has very small jowls, a sign that he's slow to learn."

"Is that why he's stubborn?" asks Geoff.

"Probably. Just like people, some learn quickly, some need more time. If you force a horse when he doesn't understand, he may become unwilling and stubborn."

"A personality evaluation will help you to get a realistic idea of your horse's abilities so you can work with him more productively. An intelligent, alert horse who learns quickly will find the constant repetition of lessons boring. He might think of ways to make the lessons more interesting: a little bucking or shying, for example. Often a horse will be punished for this, but he really didn't mean any harm. He needs a varied exercise program that fits his fast learning ability. On the other hand, you have to be more patient with a slow learner and not ask too much of him. Otherwise he may be stubborn and show you in his own way that you're going too fast for him. Even that can be misunderstood and thought of as "bad character."

I give Geoff back his photos, and the children run to the tack room to get the halters. (For my British readers, I would like to explain that in America we call the headcollar a halter, so don't be confused.) We bring a few horses in from the pasture to groom them and learn a few TTouches.

Robyn explains a few basic safety rules:

• "It's dangerous to walk into a herd of horses with grain or treats. They might fight over the treats and hurt you accidentally."

• "When you're leading a horse, use a lead rope or chain lead line with the halter. You'll be able to control the horse better and still keep a safe distance."

• "Make sure that your horse doesn't feel cornered by a more dominant horse. This is especially important when you are in front of a gate. If your horse feels threatened, he can panic and run away. You may need to keep the other horses away with a long whip or stick."

Allison stays in front of the horses to be safe. Next time she will bring her "wand" (a long whip). I am glad that Christine Schwartz, a TTeam trainer, is there to keep the other horses away from the gate.

We all go to the pasture together. The stallion watches us alertly, but he's used to seeing horses taken out of his herd. Horses often run away from people who approach from behind. They can also get scared and kick. It's better and safer to walk up to a horse from the front or the side. The horses here are no problem to catch. Shanti's chestnut even lowers his head to make it easier for her to put on the halter.

I think good manners like this should be part of every horse's training. People often come to me and complain about horses that are difficult to catch and halter. Such behavior is usually caused by bad experiences and a lack of trust in people. With the help of he TTouch and TTEAM exercises, orses learn to enjoy contact with umans and to look for it. Soon ney won't run away, but will ome to you of their own free will.

Once they know how good the 'Touch feels, they'll look forward o it. You can reward your horse vith a few TTouches when you've aught him. Then he'll come for a reat and some TTouches the next me. After a while, he will know our touch and you'll learn which 'Touches he likes best. Take a ttle time to greet your horse this vay before you take him to be roomed.

Here at the Icelandic horse farm ne horses know that they'll be vell treated and have no reason to un away from us. At the gate, we

Linda's Tip

Another way to tie a horse

You can tie and lead your horse like this:

- Hook the lead rope in the side ring of the halter. Now the horse can't pull back straight. If he does pull back, he'll have to turn his head sideways and there will be less pressure on his neck.
- You can also lead your horse with the lead rope attached to the side ring. This has proved very helpful for leading foals when they are first halter trained. Horses who have a tendency to jump and pull back will calm down more quickly when you lead them like this.
- Never tie your pony to an object which could easily break or move.

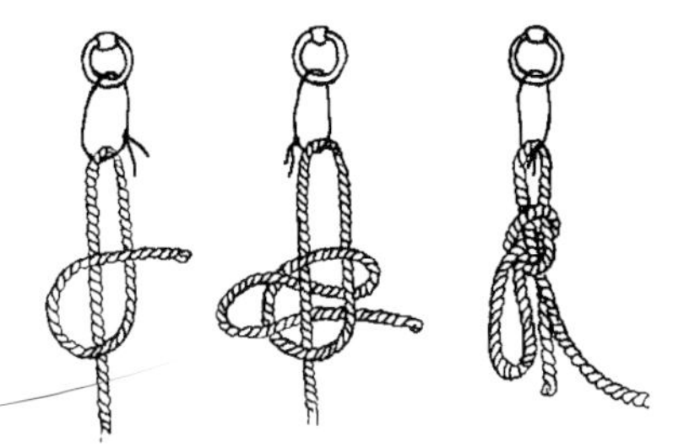

This safety knot can always be released quickly. Pass the lead rope through a piece of breakable string for added safety.

actually have to turn away some horses who want to come along.

The children tie the horses in the grooming area with a quick-release knot. They make sure to leave enough space between the horses. Horses who don't get along need to be tied far enough apart so they cannot kick or bite. Snapping teeth meant for a rival might get you instead.

Normally, horses who don't get along avoid each other in the pasture. One dominates, the other gives way. When both are tied, that isn't possible. The dominant horse might attack the other and you could be in the middle.

We tie Penni, a young gelding, a little differently from the others.

"He shies easily and will jump backwards when tied," Robyn explains.

"Is that so bad?" asks Claire.

"A horse can hurt himself that way. When he jumps back and pulls against the halter, his poll and his whole neck are strained. It's even worse if the rope breaks and he flips over backwards! I have treated many horses who were injured like this. I remember a big warmblood gelding who was in training as a dressage horse. He couldn't bend very well to the left, especially his neck, and had trouble keeping his balance. This is because he had been tied as a yearling, and hurt a vertebrae in his neck when pulling back. From then on, he swayed when he walked and couldn't move his neck well."

"He was a valuable horse and his owner had high hopes for him, but even the veterinarian couldn't help him. I showed the owner how to do some TTEAM work with him. It really helped and he

ılia grooms Drummer Boy with a ıastic curry comb and brush.

was able to be ridden and enjoy his life again. If you tie a foal for the first time without some preparation, he will fight against the pressure on his neck. If you use the TTEAM method with foals, they'll be well prepared to be tied and won't pull back."

"We don't want Penni to get hurt," says Robyn. "So we hook the lead line on the side of the halter because he's less likely to pull back when it's snapped on this way. Attach the other end of the line in a safety knot to a piece of string tied to the rail or post."

Now all the horses are tied and the children get the grooming boxes from the tack room. Before we start, we talk a little about grooming.

Grooming is more than cleaning

When you're grooming you can get acquainted with your horse and prepare him for riding. Try to find out how your horse is feeling

Shanti combs Silver's forelock carefully, making sure the mare enjoys it. Silver is pleased and closes her eyes.

Three "Groomas" with various rubber "fingers" and a "Loopa" glove are part of the TTEAM tools.

today. Is he sore or nervous, or is he relaxed? You wouldn't believe how often I see horses being groomed as though they were a rug with no feelings. I ask the children: "How can you tell if your horse doesn't like the way you're grooming him?"

"When he swishes his tail," answers Mandy.

"I know a horse who always bites the air when he's being groomed," says Talia.

"My horse won't stand still and his skin twitches," reports Shanti.

"Mine lays his ears back when I brush under his belly," says Geoff.

"And then what do you do?"

"I brush faster to get it over with!" says Allison.

"What about brushing your horse in a way that he enjoys? If your horse doesn't like a plastic curry comb, you can use a soft brush. Find out if your horse likes to be groomed softly or firmly. Has it ever occurred to you that your horse might be ticklish?"

Some of the children look at me in surprise.

"I know you're trying to do your best. Now we have the opportunity to find out what your horse really likes. A lot of very sensitive horses like being groomed with soft rubber grooming brushes. (See photo above.) There are many different kinds available, some with thick fingers and some with fine. Try them out, see how your horse responds. The grooming mitt is also very useful for sensitive parts of the body. Before you start grooming, check the entire body with your hands. This way, you can find any injuries or swellings and avoid touching them with the brush. For the mane and the tail, it's good to use a brush that doesn't pull out hair. It's best to brush in sections."

"It's important to brush your horse the way he likes to be brushed; if a horse tenses up during grooming, he'll hold his breath and tighten his back under saddle as well. This is stressful for horse and rider. A relaxed horse is not only calmer and easier to ride he'll perform better. Imagine an athlete entering a competition completely tensed up! Isn't it logical that a horse will perform better if he's relaxed at the start? Grooming doesn't just clean a horse, but also influences how he feels when you ride him and what his condition will be at the start of a competition."

"If your horse doesn't like being groomed try slowing down your strokes and breathe rhythmically with each stroke of the brush. Avoid making circles with the curry comb on a tense horse."

Linda's Tip

Mud on a wet coat

Keep a bucket with dry sawdust in the tack room. (You can buy it in a pet shop. Make sure that it hasn't been treated with wood preservatives.) If a horse is very wet and dirty, rub damp sawdust into the mud on his coat. It draws the moisture and the dirt will come out easily.

Linda's Tip

Picking up your horse's feet

• Does this sound familiar? A horse won't pick up his hoof willingly, so you lean into his shoulder to get him to shift his weight to the other side. The only problem is, you throw the horse off balance. The goal of TTEAM work is to bring the horse into balance!

Now try the following method: place your thumb and index finger on either side of the big tendon above the fetlock joint, then apply light alternating pressure while pulling upward with a slide of your fingernails. Your horse should lift up his foot. It's important to press slightly upward and release, with a short pause between signals.

• Some horses have the annoying habit of jerking a leg away after

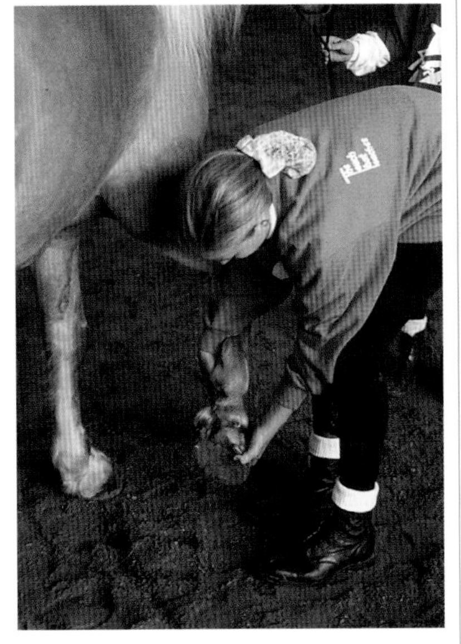

you've picked it up. To overcome this, immediately you pick up the leg, hold it slightly below the height of the opposite knee grasping the side of the hoof in one hand and the fetlock with the other. Circle the hoof two or three times in both directions while spiralling it down to the ground. Rest the toe on the ground about eight inches back. This exercise relaxes the shoulder and forearm muscles. After he gets used to it, his balance will improve, which makes it easier for him to stand on three legs.

Angie says

Did you know that many horses are ticklish? If a horse won't stand still while you're grooming him, if he swishes his tail and is nervous, you may be touching a ticklish place. Be patient! Take the time to find where your horse is ticklish or sensitive, where he likes a stiffer brush, and where he prefers a softer brush. Imagine someone scraping your spine with a curry comb! Well? It hurts! Please use a curry comb only on a very dirty horse with a thick coat, and not on his face, legs or over protruding bones. If you pay attention to your horse's reactions, you'll soon find out what he likes.

Regular cleaning of the hooves keeps them healthy. It's important to point the hoof pick away from you and the horse's leg.

Shanti brushes the tail in small portions and is careful not to pull out hair.

Bodywork with TTouch

The horses are groomed. Claire brushes the mane one more time, till she is pleased. "Linda, how exactly do you do the TTouch?"

Years ago a participant in a clinic once asked me a similar question. Her name was Wendy. She owned a nine-year-old Thoroughbred mare who didn't like to be touched. The mare threw her head around, wouldn't stand still and pinned her ears back. When I worked on her she calmed down, but when Wendy tried it, she showed her dislike very clearly.

"Just what is it you do with your fingers? When you do it, it always looks so easy, but I don't know what my fingers should do!" she asked me.

Without thinking about it I heard myself say: "You simply put your hand on the horse and push the skin with the pads of your fingers in a small circle." And it worked! In a few minutes her horse relaxed and started to enjoy her touch. The mare stopped moving around and pinning her ears back.

Geoff looks at me in amazement. "And you had never done the circles before?"

"No! I don't know myself how I thought of it. I think the words came from heaven. Maybe Angie whispered them in my ear. I work intuitively, from my feelings, but I also use my intelligence."

When you learn TTEAM you develop your intuition and your mind at the same time. After the experience with Wendy I started to experiment with the circles. It took many years to develop the TTouch the way I teach it today.

I still remember the first horse I worked with using my Feldenkrais training. She was a sixteen-year-old Arabian mare owned by my neighbor, Ted. She had been a broodmare all her life, had never been ridden and didn't like people very much. This was always very obvious when Ted tried to catch her. She ran from him every time and it took him ages every evening until he finally had her in the barn. I decided to move her body gently in unusual ways to see if I could change her behavior. But would this work? I had never tried it. But the method worked so well for humans why shouldn't it work with a horse? I remembered what my grandfather Will always used to say about the herbal medicines he made for his racehorses: "It can't hurt!" And weren't the horses he trained so successful because his grooms rubbed them down for half-an-hour with their hands?

It was worth a try, I actually

At a glance

The TTouch

What is it?

Special circular movements made with the hands. I've given each TTouch a name taken from the animal kingdom.

What is for?

The TTouch has many helpful effects. With TTouches, a horse learns to overcome fear and better understand what you ask of him. With the TTouch you can do something nice for your horse, relax him and be a better friend.

What does it do?

With the help of the TTouch your horse will feel his own body better. You can visualize that you are waking up each cell in his body with your TTouches. It's as if little electric lights are turning on in the area where you are working. Your horse will become more aware of himself. As a result, he will feel better; be more balanced and athletic; calmer; more cooperative; and perform to his utmost.

Caution!

It's very important to keep your hands softly rounded like a big paw with enough pressure to push the skin in a circle. Many people make the mistake of sliding their fingers over the skin. If you stiffen your fingers and hold your breath, the TTouch will be uncomfortable for you and your horse.

ouldn't wait to put my theories o work.

So I did whatever came to my nind: I worked on her ears, noved her legs and her tail and vorked her mouth. She liked vhat I was doing and became ery quiet and relaxed. This was a irst step and I didn't expect more.

But Ted called me a few days ater to tell me that the mare was otally transformed. He didn't eed to chase her anymore, ecause she stood waiting at the ate for him every evening. In her tall she didn't rush to eat her eed as usual, but stood by him, vaiting for him to do the earwork vith her. A single treatment had hanged her entire relationship vith humans profoundly.

"So what do I do?" Claire wants o try the TTouch.

"It's really simple. For the ircular TTouches you imagine the ound face of a clock on your orse's body, half-an-inch in iameter. Your hand should be ghtly curved to keep the joints of our fingers flexible. Push the kin with three fingers, keeping onstant pressure in a clockwise irection and let the little finger ollow. Anchor your thumb a ouple of inches away from the ther fingers. Make sure your ngers don't just slide over the air, but gently hold the skin and nove it in a circle, one and a uarter times around. This means ou push the skin around the ircle once, until you come to six o'clock again. Go past six o'clock to eight, then slide your fingers lightly to start the next circle. It's important to only go round one and a quarter circles in one place. If you make several circles on the same spot, the result is not the same. Make each circle in a new place to increase your horse's feeling of his body. Let your intuition guide you. With a little practice your hands will know where to make the next circle. You can also make the circles in parallel lines to your horse's topline. If you do this you can also connect each circle with a little slide to the next circle."

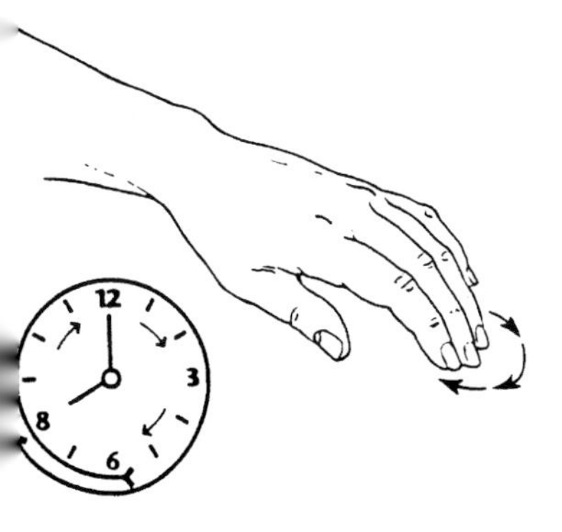

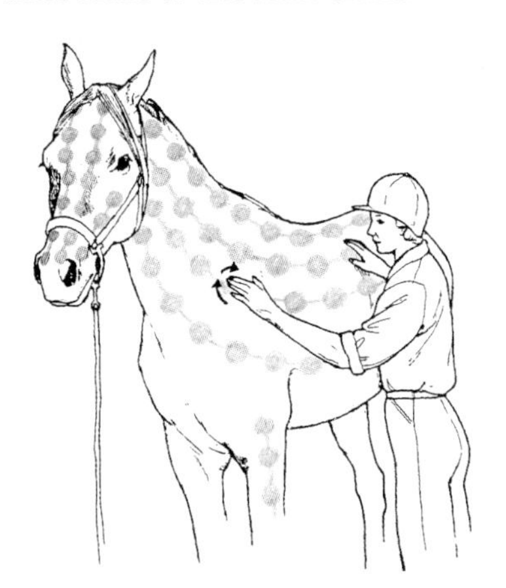

Claire is already doing the circles on her horse's neck. "Can I also do them counterclockwise?'

"Usually I do the circles clockwise. That strengthens the body and increases the awareness. It can also reduce nervousness, stress and soreness."

"But if you have a horse who doesn't like to be touched or is sore, try making the circles counterclockwise, to see if he likes it better."

Talia has been listening attentively. "Do you really think we can do this?" Her voice sounds uncertain and she's looking at her hands skeptically.

"You certainly have a special gift...", she continues.

I hold my hands next to hers.

"You can do the TTouch with your hands just as well as I can! There are always people who think that I have special healing powers or even a secret. If there is a secret, it lies in the roundness and smoothness of the circles and in my ability to listen to my inner voice. You can do the same thing – anyone can learn the TTouch. Be

The TTouch is no secret: anyone can learn it. I am showing Shanti how to do Raccoon TTouches on the horse's face.

confident. Your hands are just as gifted as mine and you can do a lot of good for your horse. All it takes is some practice. And that's what we're going to do now."

"Let's start with the **Clouded Leopard:** you can do this TTouch all over your horse's body. Your hand rests on your horse's body with fingers lightly curved. Your fingers push the skin around the clock for one and a quarter circles. Feel how your fingers work together. Remember to anchor the thumb. While you make the circles keep your breathing rhythmic. It's common to concentrate on the movement so much that you forget to breathe. Breathing will keep your hand and fingers, as well as your arm and shoulder, soft and movable."

Soon everyone is busy practicing the Clouded Leopard. After a little while they're ready for the next TTouch, the **Lying Leopard:**

"For this TTouch your hand flattens a little. Your fingers stretch out more, but are still lightly curved. I imagine that my hand is the body of a leopard. My fingers are his forelegs. Now he stretches them out to lie down. A larger area of my palm touches the skin and allows for a warmer contact. The Clouded Leopard increases a horse's awareness, the Lying Leopard has a calming effect. No matter which TTouch you use, remember to keep your breathing quiet and rhythmic. If your horse is nervous you can make the circles slightly faster. When your horse relaxes you can slow them down."

The horses obviously enjoy the TTouch. Some are so relaxed that they are resting one hind leg, others lick their lips contentedly. The horses' eyes are soft, their breathing is quiet. Even Penni's eyes are half-closed; he's standing quietly with a low head. The children are working in pairs: one holds the horse and works on the ears while the other one is practicing the TTouch. (If you are working alone you can tie your horse or teach him to stand untied.) The one holding the horse can also do some TTouches on the face. The Lying Leopard TTouch and the **Raccoon TTouch**

"For the Lying Leopard you stretch out your fingers a little for a warmer contact."

At a glance

Clouded Leopard

What is it? This is the basic TTouch position for all over the horse's body. Years ago I used the TTouch on a clouded leopard in the Los Angeles Zoo. She had been taken away from her mother too soon and consequently, had not nursed long enough. She was nervous and neurotic, licking the bars of her cage and being generally very restless. This leopard's ancestors lived in high, cloud-covered mountains in northern India – hence the name. This TTouch can be as powerful as a leopard and yet as gentle as a cloud. Although I met this leopard just once, I think of her often.

What is it for? It increases a horse's self-confidence; helps with back pain, tension, muscle pain, over-sensitivity, as well as reducing stress.

What does it do? A horse will be calmer, have a better awareness of his body, be more relaxed and cooperate more willingly.

Caution! Watch your horse's reaction! If he seems uncomfortable, try either lightening or increasing the pressure. You can also try the same TTouch in a different area or change to another TTouch. Make sure you are actually moving the skin in a circle rather than just rubbing over the hair.

At a glance

Lying Leopard

What is it? This is a less invasive variation of the Clouded Leopard TTouch and should be used if a horse seems too sensitive for the Clouded Leopard. The Lying Leopard was named after a snow leopard I met at the Zurich Zoo. He was suffering from a respiratory illness and was expected to die. I was asked to work on him. I put the baby leopard on my lap and worked on him with small circles and the warmth of my hands over every inch of his body. He began eating soon after and was on the mend by the next day!

What is it for? To reduce tension, nervousness, stress, and helps horses get over their resistance when being cinched or girthed. It's gentle enough to use on an area that has been injured.

What does it do? The flattened hand makes for a larger area of warm contact. This will help your horse relax.

Caution! Make sure you keep your wrists straight and fingers soft and flexible even though your hand is nearly flat. This protects your finger joints from becoming tired or strained.

re perfect for that.

For the Raccoon TTouch the ingertips make a light contact. 'our fingernails don't touch your ıorse. Remember to breathe while 'ou are making small circles lowly! You can work on or round swellings and bruises or ven on painful areas or injuries vith this light TTouch.

"Does a horse feel such a gentle 'Touch?"asks Geoff. "I can't magine it has any effect at all."

"You'd be surprised! When you ıse the Raccoon TTouch to work round the eyes, your horse will alm down a lot. Working on his ace will increase his trust in you."

"Do you remember the story of ıe old horseman in

Raccoon TTouches around the eyes relax and calm the horse. This little gray mare trusts Shanti.

Farmington?"asks Robyn.

Of course! I was giving a clinic for Farmington ranchers and horse breeders. Some had brought their own horses for me to work with. After the clinic one of the ranchers came to me:

"I don't quite know what to think of your method," he started out. "But I have a horse at home I'd like to try the TTouch on."

Linda's Tip

Suggestions for the TTouch

I've written down a few important things for you to keep in mind while doing TTouches.

- Your horse should wear a well-fitting halter (headcollar) with a lead rope or a chain lead line attached correctly to the halter (headcollar) (see page 42). If you don't have a helper to hold the horse you may tie him with the lead rope, but never with the chain lead line.
- Your breathing is very important – practice breathing calmly and evenly. Both you and your horse will be tense when you hold your breath.
- Keep the joints in your hand and fingers soft and rounded while doing TTouches.
- Make your circles really round with a steady, flowing motion.
- It's easiest for your back if you stand with your feet under your hips and your knees lightly bent. You will also be able get out of the way more quickly if your horse gets frightened and makes a sudden move to the side.
- In the beginning, especially, it is best to work in a quiet, undisturbed place your horse knows and feels safe in. Your horse can feel the TTouches and enjoy them more when he's relaxed. A quiet place is also less distracting for you. His box stall is a good choice.

"Why didn't you bring your horse?" I wondered. "It would have certainly been interesting to work with him. What kind of a horse is he?"

"Well, you know," he said with a grin, "he's a Quarter Horse gelding and I thought I'd better leave him at home. I didn't want to embarrass you. He isn't a horse for a lady. I was sure you wouldn't be able to handle him and I wanted to spare you that. He's very stubborn and doesn't want anything to do with people. He is sixteen years old and the only way I can catch him is with a lasso. It's hard work to put a halter on him. But once you're on his back he's a super roping horse. After the horses I have seen you work with this weekend, now I wish I had brought him."

I laughed, wished him luck and was surprised when he called me the next day.

"You won't believe what happened," he said. "When I got home I lassoed my hard-headed gelding. I didn't really believe that these circles would do any good, but I thought I would just give it a try. I certainly didn't work longer than ten minutes, just did those tiny circles on the face, and then I wanted to turn him out to pasture again. But he wouldn't go! He followed me to the gate and tried to come out of the pasture with me. It's unbelievable, all because of some circles on his face!"

"Can I do the circles on the legs also?" asks Allison.

"Of course! A nice TTouch for the legs is the **Python Lift.**"

"That's the one you named after Joyce, the Burmese python, isn't it?" adds my niece Mandy, who knows the story already.

"That's right. When I do this TTouch I often think of Joyce."

I demonstrate the Python Lift on Mandy. "On a person you place both hands around the leg, just beneath the knee. On a horse you start a few inches below the elbow. Now slowly push the skin slightly upward. Use just enough pressure to keep your hands from sliding. Now pause for about four seconds and then slowly return the skin to the starting point. Slide your hands down a few inches to do the next Python Lift. You can use Python Lifts down the entire leg."

"The horses in my riding school pick up their feet as soon as you touch their leg," says Talia.

Many horses have that habit if they are nervous about having their legs touched or if you squeeze or push the skin upwards too much. Maybe your horse thinks you want him to pick up

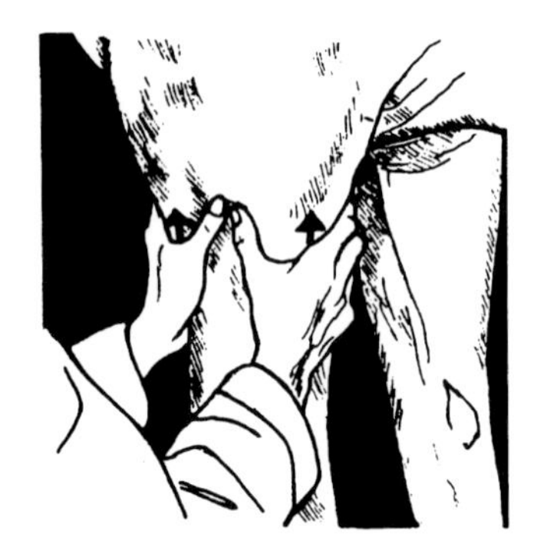

You start the Python Lifts below the elbow.

his foot. It's useful to teach your horse to stand still when you touch his legs. What if he had a wound that needed treatment? It's important that your horse stands still and doesn't pick up his foot when you are applying any kind of wrap or bandage. It's important to teach your horse to wait for your signals or aids before he acts.

At a glance

Raccoon TTouch

What is it?
Raccoon TTouches are tiny circles done with the tips of the fingers. Raccoons make tiny movements with their quick and nimble little paws when eating their food.That's why I named this TTouch after them.

What is it for?
It's good for the treatment of bruises and swelling around injuries to speed up healing. You can use it all over a horse's face to develop trust.

What does it do?
It helps swellings go down and promotes healing by increasing circulation.

Caution!
Even if you are only using light pressure it may be uncomfortable for your horse to be touched directly on a painful area. Always watch your horse's reaction and be ready to change to a different TTouch or place.

Linda's Tip

TTouch also helps humans

Try out the TTouch on yourself or on a friend. Then you can feel on your own body how the TTouch feels. TTouch is not only effective on horses, but also beneficial to humans. I have had many good results with it. In the case of a headache, for example, you can do tiny, slow Raccoon circles on the inside of the ear and the rim. Or, if you are nervous or fearful before a test at school or at a horse show, you can work your own ears. Place your thumb behind your ear. Make sliding upward strokes with your forefinger on the front side over every little bit of your ear.

'his starts with picking up the ɜet and goes all the way to hanging gaits in a competition. If your horse has difficulty tanding still you can stroke his ɜgs with the wand and then do onnected circles in a row down he leg. Then do a few Python .ifts. Praise your horse for

At a glance

Python Lift

What is it?

This is a TTouch that I used to help a Burmese python called Joyce and then named it after her. Joyce was living in a California wildlife park suffering from bouts of pneumonia. On horses you can use the Python Lift very effectively on their backs, necks and legs.

What is it for?

It helps tight muscles, spasms and is especially useful for horses who shy, stumble, or have trouble keeping their balance in a trailer.

What does it do?

The Python Lift relaxes and calms a nervous horse, It increases circulation and improves balance and stride. When done on a horse's legs it makes him more sure-footed specifically and more confident overall.

Caution!

If you lift the skin too quickly or too much, press too hard or release too suddenly, your horse may tense up and not stand quietly.

standing still.

Robyn's horses know Python Lifts and stand quietly. That makes it easy for the children to learn and practice the TTouch. Once they have all tried it I call the group together.

"Now I'll show you another TTouch. It works well with the others and is called **The Lick of the Cow's Tongue**."

"Put your slightly curved hand under your horse's belly, with the fingers spread slightly apart. Now gently slide your hand across the belly and over your horse's back. Half-way up the side turn your hand so that your fingers now point upwards in the direction you are moving. This long TTouch goes all the way up to the topline. This is also a nice TTouch for the shoulder or croup of your horse. Make sure you're using the heel of your hand as well as your fingers. While you do this TTouch starting from the belly, the other hand stays under the belly. When doing this TTouch on the shoulder or neck, the other hand stays at the chest. Do this TTouch alternately with both hands on the croup. It's a lot of fun to learn to do this sweeping motion from your feet and pelvis so that your arm won't get tired and you'll be better balanced."

After a few minutes of practice Shanti has a question: "The Icelandics aren't so tall, I can just reach up to their backs," she says. "But how should I do the Lick of the Cow's Tongue with a big horse? I'm much too small!"

Short people can work on tall horses with the help of a bale of straw or hay. "I can't always reach the back of some of the tall horses either. So I use a bale or a strong box to stand on," I explain to Shanti. "Whatever you use it has to be something you can stand on

At a glance

Lick of the Cow's Tongue

What is it?

Long, diagonal strokes done from the belly to the back. This feeling reminds me of the times when I was licked by a cow as a child. I think of my bull calf 'Dale' when I use this TTouch. If you've never been licked by a cow, perhaps you've had a similar feeling from being licked by a cat.

What is it for?

It is soothing for sore, over-worked muscles after a hard workout. It also helps to loosen the muscles of horses who are stiff or tight in their backs.

What does it do?

This TTouch helps a horse feel connected through the whole body. This better sense of his body improves a horse's self-confidence, coordination, balance and gait. In addition, the circulation of blood in the muscles increases, promoting a quicker and longer-lasting recovery after hard work.

Caution!

Some horses don't like this TTouch if their abdominal muscles are tight. They may kick at your hand on their belly as if they are kicking at a fly. In these cases you can use the Lying Leopard TTouch until they learn to accept, and like, contact in this area.

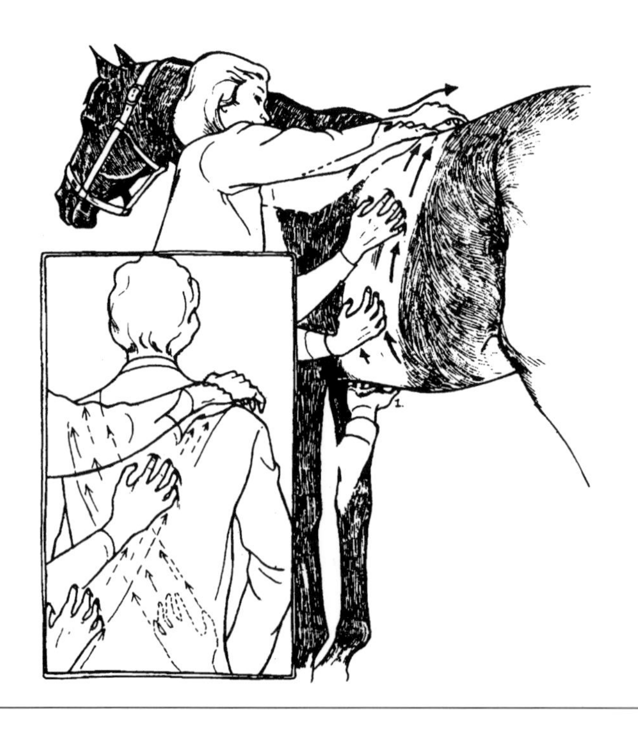

ıfely. If you do use a box make .ıre to put it down with the open de to the ground, otherwise our horse could step into it by ccident."

"Lunch time!" we hear them ılling from the house. But before e go to eat we turn the horses ut again so that they can move round freely and graze.

Ihe **Ear TTouch** is one of the ıost important TTouches," I xplain to the children when we ave brought the horses in from ıe field again after lunch. When I emonstrated the Ear TTouch ıany years ago at a horse fair in ermany, an elderly English entleman came to me: "It used to e a tradition to rub the ears of ıe carriage horses in England uring their breaks," he said. "It elped them to recover from hard ork."

eoff's first attempt at stroking the ear. ually, we stand in front of the horse do the Ear TTouch.

I've had the same experience. In any cases the Ear TTouch has orked very well to calm nervous orses. The Ear TTouch has oven to be helpful even with orses who are colicking, are in ock from injury or are completely exhausted.

Almost thirty years ago I was able to save the life of my favorite mare, Bint Gulida. She colicked so severely that the vet gave up hope and recommended we put her down. But I didn't want to give up. Gulida's ears were very wet and ice cold so I worked and rubbed them until they were warm and dry. You can imagine how happy I was when Gulida, against all odds, recovered and got well. Of course, you need to call the vet in any case of colic but until he or she arrives you can work your horse's ears.

You can reach your horse's ears most easily when you stand in front of him. But that's not the only reason: your horse learns to lower his head when you ask him to with a gentle tug on the lead line. This lowering of the head is a sign of trust. In his body language the horse is telling you; "I trust you and I am willing to do what you ask of me."

To do the Ear TTouch one hand holds the halter or headcollar on one side of the noseband while the other hand strokes the ear on the opposite side, from the base of the ear to the tip. In the case of shock or colic, make sure you press firmly as you slide off the tip of the ear while you wait for the vet. (You can also make tiny connected Raccoon TTouches in lines from the base of the ear to its tip to improve the general health of your horse and help him with back pain, arthritis or stiffness.)

Next I show the children the **Mouth TTouch.** It is very useful in many ways, but especially to influence your horse's emotions. It helps especially with horses

At a glance

Ear TTouch

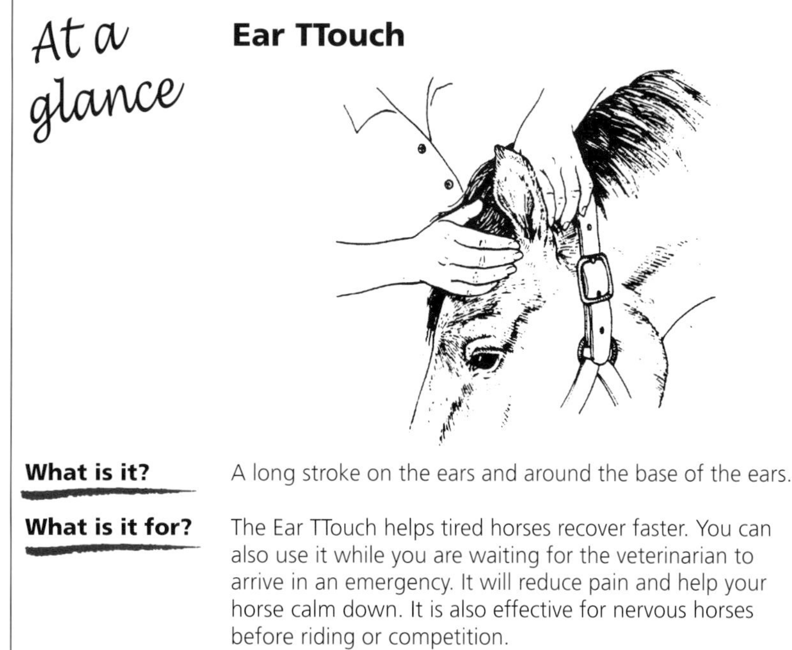

What is it? A long stroke on the ears and around the base of the ears.

What is it for? The Ear TTouch helps tired horses recover faster. You can also use it while you are waiting for the veterinarian to arrive in an emergency. It will reduce pain and help your horse calm down. It is also effective for nervous horses before riding or competition.

What does it do? There are many acupressure points at the base and at the tip of the ear. When you stimulate these points with TTouches you provide many beneficial effects over the entire horse. This stimulation especially helps digestion and breathing.

Caution! Ear work is usually done standing in front of your horse. Make sure you're giving your horse enough space – if you're standing too close he may tell you with a push of his nose!

1 "Your horse is holding his head too high for the Ear TTouch. You have to stand on your tip toes to even reach the ears!"

2 "Let me show you how you can make it easier for yourself. You hold his noseband and ask your horse to lower his head."

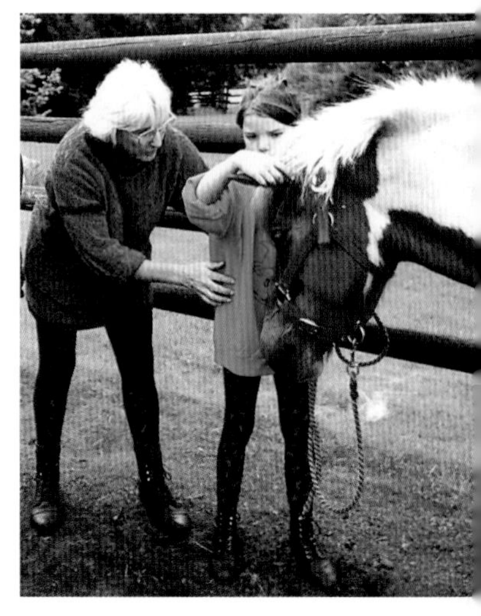

3 "Now you can reach the ears without difficulty! If you face the horse and stand directly in front it will be even easier."

At a glance

Mouth TTouch

What is it?
Various touches in and around the mouth, on the gums and the lips of the horse.

Tools
If your horse's gums are dry you can use water to wet your hands. It's helpful to have small bucket of water handy to wet your fingers when necessary.

What is it for?
For horses who are nervous, tense, stubborn, who bite, or are resistant to training. It is also a very useful preparatory treatment before worming, floating (rasping) teeth, or bitting young horses.

What does it do?
It works on the part of the brain that controls emotion, thus improving behavior.

Caution!
Be extra careful not to get bitten! The illustrations show you where to put your fingers. Slide your fingers back and forth on the gums under the upper or lower lip.

who are nervous, stubborn, mean or fearful, or who seem uninterested in people. Once I had a yearling in one of my clinics who constantly nipped at and bit people. Her owner had tried all kinds of things to stop her, including hitting her with a whip but nothing had worked so far. I showed the audience how to work the gums of the filly's mouth. After the clinic she stopped nipping altogether.

Unfortunately many foals are not well educated from the beginning. Often young foals are allowed to nibble at their owner because people think it's cute. The horse learns to treat humans like playmates. As he grows stronger the playful nibbling suddenly becomes nipping and biting. Now everyone is shocked! The horse is a biter! And it is the humans who have taught him do so!

When you do the mouth work you stand slightly behind your horse's head, facing in the same direction. Hold the halter with one hand while the other hand does Lying Leopard TTouches on the outside of the upper mouth, the lips and the chin. When your orse accepts your touch, lift the orner of the upper lip with your humb and slide your fingers ack and forth over the gums nd above the teeth. You can vork the gums under the lower p, too.

Of course you must be very areful! You know that horses not nly have front teeth, but also big holars in the back. Keep your ngers out of reach of the teeth nd make sure they don't ccidentally slide in between hem.

"What can I do when my horse oesn't allow his mouth to be ouched?"

"In that case you can start by

You can work the nostrils with a friend...

...or alone.

lia carefully slides her fingers on the ums under the upper lip of the horse.

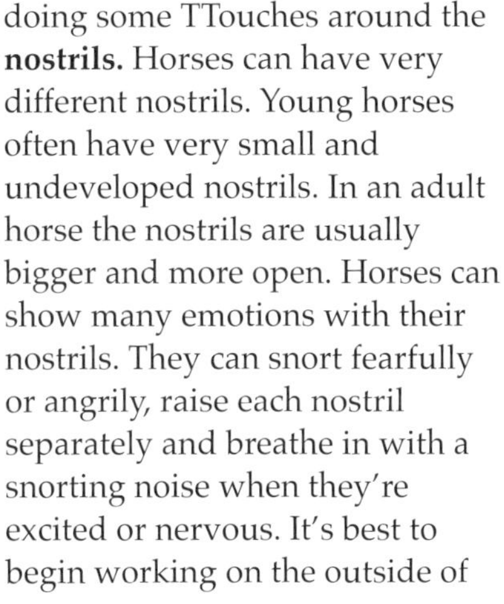

doing some TTouches around the **nostrils.** Horses can have very different nostrils. Young horses often have very small and undeveloped nostrils. In an adult horse the nostrils are usually bigger and more open. Horses can show many emotions with their nostrils. They can snort fearfully or angrily, raise each nostril separately and breathe in with a snorting noise when they're excited or nervous. It's best to begin working on the outside of the nostrils, moving the edges between your thumb and bent index finger. This will teach your horse to be patient and make it much easier for the vet to put a tube down his esophagus in case of a colic emergency."

"It's fun for two people to work the horse's nostrils, but you can easily do it alone. Stand in front or to the side of your horse's head and start with one nostril while holding the halter with your other hand. Move the nostril between the thumb and forefinger. After a while you can slide your thumb a little deeper into your horse's nostril. Horses usually like a firm touch on their nostrils. They don't like to be tickled."

Some horses hold tension in their muzzle and nostrils. By working their nostrils you can show them that they can also be soft and flexible. This also improves a horse's breathing. Once your horse accepts the work with one nostril you can work the second one. Sometimes you can even work both nostrils simultaneously and do circles on them.

The young mare enjoys the Mouth TTouch. She is so pleased that she closes her eyes and stretches her neck to make it even easier for Talia to do the TTouch on her gums.

A visit to the Arabian farm

"Today we're going to the Arabians!" Claire is excited. I want the children to get to know different breeds of horses, so we gratefully accepted the invitation of Mrs Goertz to visit her breeding farm "Asmura Arabians". A short drive brings us to the beautifully located mountain ranch. Majestic pine trees grow along the road and elegant horses are grazing in their rolling pastures. The sun is shining in a blue sky while high above the trees a few small white clouds float.

Sheila Goertz is waiting for us in front of her stable and greets us heartily. She gives us a short tour of her facilities and introduces us to her horses. She breeds Spanish Arabians and is rightfully proud of her noble horses. She suggests we work with a two-year-old named Asmura Casamira. The graceful, friendly filly is not yet trained to ride. Mrs Goertz is giving her the time she needs to fully develop and mature, mentally and physically, and will not ride her until she is three and a half years old.

The children lead Casamira from the barn to a big field where we will work with her. It is Casamira's first experience with the TTouch and she enjoys it from the very first moment.

"Where do we start?" asks Shanti.

"I suggest doing some exploratory TTouches all over her body. Notice cold and warm areas, if you can find a ticklish place and where she really likes to be touched. Can you touch her anywhere? Her face, her mouth, her ears? Is she standing still while you touch all four legs?"

The children carefully examine Casamira's body, exchange their observations and get to know the young mare better.

"What can I do when my horse doesn't like to have his mane pulled?" asks Talia.

I know the problem from working with many performance horses in competition stables.

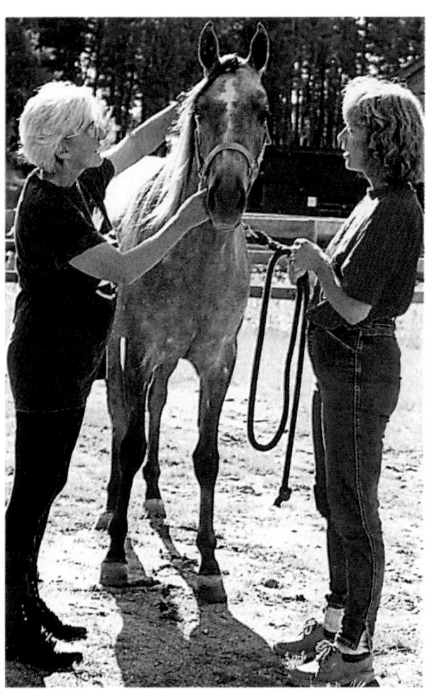

Sheila Goertz introduces me to her two-year-old purebred Spanish Arabian filly Casamira. The head already shows me that the mare is friendly, intelligent and loves people.

It's easier together! Shanti and Talia are leading Casamira to the field.

Angie says

Are there some children in your class who are bigger and stronger than others? Should their parents take them out of school and set them to hard labor, just because they seem almost full grown? Of course not! Unfortunately, many horses are ridden much too early because they are big. But their joints and bones are not ready to carry the weight of a rider, especially in tight turns or when they are being lunged a lot. Most horses may be carefully started under saddle at age three, but some breeds – small ones like Icelandics and large warmbloods need more time to develop and are better started under saddle at four or five years of age. Please be patient. Your horse will thank you with a long, healthy life.

asamira likes the TTouch at the base of er ears. Mandy works with oncentration and great sensitivity.

Iost people pull the mane ownwards to shorten it, and that an really hurt.
Mandy and Casamira show how ou can prepare your horse for aving his mane pulled. Place our hands on top of the neck bout four inches apart, with the humbs on one side and the ngers on the other. Hold the crest rmly and push your hands owards each other without iding them along the crest. Hold or a few seconds and then pull our hands apart, stretching the skin on the crest. Move both hands to another area on the neck and repeat this TTouch there. I call this TTouch the **Inchworm.** The horse's head should be level, just like the horse in the photos.

When you have done the Inchworm all along the neck, separate the mane in strands to the left and right of the neck and gently pull them down by sliding your hands down the hair. I call this doing "slides". Then take the strands and lift them while sliding your hands up the hair. (This mane or hair work is also wonderful for humans and helps with headaches. You can try it on yourself or on a friend.) For horses it is not only a useful preparation before pulling the mane, but it also relaxes the entire neck, shoulders and back. Many horses are very tight and sore in the neck, especially when they have to do a lot of collected work which can block circulation. Lengthening and stretching relaxes the neck and increases blood flow and circulation.

One of the grooms walks by and watches our work with Casamira for a while. "Why do you do all this?" he wants to know.

"Well?" I look at the children. "Why do we?"

"It's fun for us and nice for the horses," says Geoff.

"To make the horses feel better," is Shanti's answer.

"So they trust us more," Claire says.

Pulling the mane

Often a horse doesn't like to have his mane pulled so he fights it for a good reason: when you pull down on the hair it can hurt!

You can make it more acceptable for your horse. Prepare him for having his mane pulled by parting his mane in two-inch sections to the left and right and do slides from the crest to the end of the clumps of hair. To shorten the mane you then lift a few strands of hair upwards, select a few to pull, push the rest downward and then pull the few out with a quick pluck, straight up. This method doesn't hurt your horse.

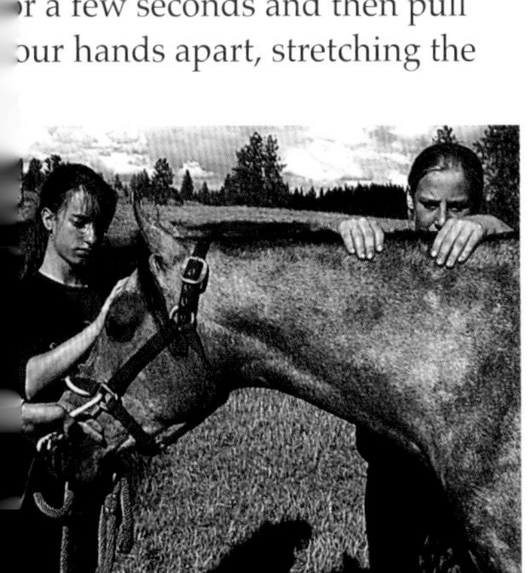

do the Inchworm you push the hands gether and release in short intervals.

Mandy carefully parts the mane a few strands at a time. Casamira lowers her head – she trusts Mandy.

The fingers glide up the strands of hair. From this position it won't be a problem to pull the mane.

Horses often like to have several people work on them. Talia is doing Lying Leopard TTouches on the face, Mandy does the Inchworm on the neck and Shanti starts with some Tail TTouches.

And Mandy adds: "They become more athletic."

"That's right. With the TTouch a horse develops a new awareness for his entire body: his ears, nostrils, mouth, legs, back, neck, belly and tail. His stride lengthens, his balance improves and he feels more confident. He can do what is asked of him more easily. He will be more successful in competitions, improve his gaits and be able to jump higher and wider. And we'll have a new relationship with our horse – he becomes our friend!"

You don't need strength to do the TTouch and it doesn't require much time. Five minutes is often all it takes to relax and bring a horse who already knows the TTouch into top form before a competition or connect with him before a ride.

Interestingly, the TTEAM work keeps developing. While I am working with horses they often inspire me to try something new and sometimes that leads to developing a new TTouch. That's what happened when I worked with Rembrandt Borbet, Nicole Uphoff-Becker's legendary dressage horse. For years the two rode from one victory to the next: the European Championships, the World Championships, and the Olympic Games, where they won two gold medals. While I was working with "Remmi", Nicole's nickname for the gelding, I crossed my hands at the wrists and did Clouded Leopard circles simultaneously with both hands. By crossing the hands I could cover a larger area and it gave me a very balanced feeling. You can also try this TTouch with a friend and practice on one another. Most humans find it to be just as pleasant and revitalizing as horses do. The way I'm holding my hands reminds me of a hawk, who sails through the air with outspread wings – this is why I call this TTouch the **Kestrel TTouch.**

I take Casamira's tail and do slides down single strands of hair. This is a very useful TTouch. "This year I worked with Grazioso, a young horse owned by German dressage rider and Olympic medal winner Klaus Balkenhol. The gelding was very nervous and would shy from any sound or movement in the audience. He

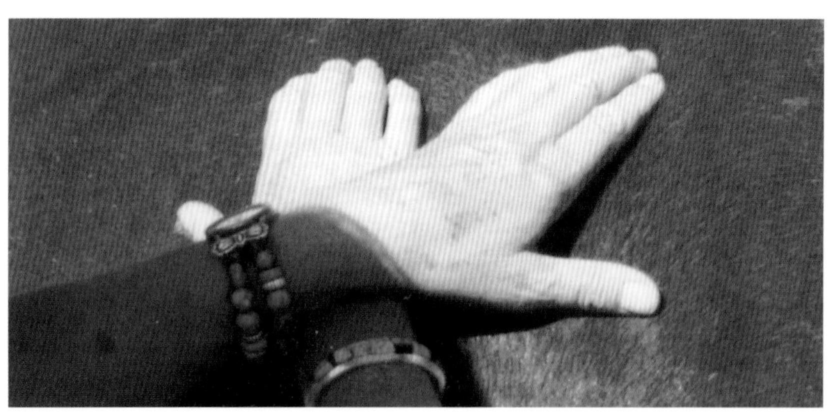

I developed the Kestrel TTouch in my work with heavily-muscled sport horses. I cross my hands at the wrists and can cover more area. Crossing your wrists will improve your coordination, too.

Angie says

Humans are lucky! When a human being becomes a great athlete, he has helpers who care for his physical well-being. He gets rubdowns and is well taken care of by trainers. Other people treat themselves to a relaxing massage when they are tense, have a headache or a sore back – well, horses can benefit from this kind of treatment too. TTouches are so enjoyable for horses: they can relax, learn to make better use of their bodies and carry riders with less effort! Some horses are super athletes on four legs. They need the TTouch to perform the fantastic feats we ask of them.

ad a hard time concentrating and ad not been placed at any of his ix competitions. I went with the alkenhol family to a big dressage how and worked on Grazioso efore his test. I worked over his vhole body for an hour earlier in ne day, but just before his test I id Python Lifts, Ear TTouches nd hairslides on his tail for fifteen ninutes, helpful for horses who hy or are afraid of noises and novement from behind. When razioso entered the arena, for the rst time he was concentrating, legant and didn't shy once. He von the competition by many oints.

There are four different ways of oing the **Tail TTouch**:

• Raccoon TTouch: Begin by tanding to the side of the indquarters for safety. When orses get scared they may kick ackwards, but only rarely will ney kick to the side. Stand behind our horse only when you are ure that he enjoys the Tail TTouch nd won't kick.

For horses who clamp their tail, tart with small Raccoon TTouches round the side and underneath ne base of the tail. This helps orses who hold their tail tightly et go and lift their tail.

• Rotating the tail: Standing lightly to the left side pick up the ail with your right hand two-nirds of the way down the tail one, with your left hand upporting the tail from underneath about eight inches from the end. Now gently push the tail inwards and upwards with your right hand. Make sure the tail is arched, then rotate it several times in each direction.

At a glance

Tail TTouch

What is it?
TTouches on, and movements with, a horse's tail.

What is it for?
This TTouch is beneficial for horses who are afraid of noises and movements from behind, who kick at other horses, or kick while being trailered. It's also good for horses with sore backs.

What does it do?
The tailbone is the continuation of the spine. By gently pulling and releasing the tail the muscles will soften, from the hindquarters through the back and all the way into the neck. Often your horse will turn around, look at you and take a deep breath when you release the tail!

Caution!
Only stand behind a horse when you are certain that he won't kick. If you are in doubt, just do the movements you can do easily and safely at the side.

• Flexing the tail: Stand directly behind your horse (only when you are sure your horse is safe, otherwise stay to the side). Place your hands around the tail with your fingers under the tail bone and your thumbs on top. Gently flex the tailbone forward and back. Imagine that the tail is like a string of pearls. Gently move from one vertebra or "pearl" to the next.

• "Weighting" the tail: Only do this movement if your horse is really quiet and dependable. Stand behind your horse. Hold one hand halfway down the tailbone, and the other near the end of the tailbone. When you work with a very large horse you can put one hand on the tail bone and hold the hair of the tail with the other hand. Stand with one foot forward and the other foot back in my position shown in the photos on page 34. Now slowly shift your weight to your back foot and pull the tail gently and steadily. Hold for a few seconds and release gradually. Keep in mind that the tail bone is a continuation of the spine. This is why work on the tail affects the back and the neck all the way up to the poll. When you pull slowly you influence the entire spine and often your horse will take a deep breath. It is important to release gradually. If you let go too suddenly you will cause your horse to tense his back muscles.

The Tail TTouches also increase

a horse's self-confidence. Once I was called by an Arabian breeder to have a look at one of his promising young colts – a future stallion prospect. The horse was elegant, but very timid. In the herd he was the lowest horse on the totem pole and did not display the self-confidence and proud temperament his breeder expected of a herd sire. I noticed that the colt carried his tail tightly pressed against his hindquarters and not proudly arched like most Arabians. I worked on him for only two ten-minute sessions and the results were astounding. After I did all the Tail TTouches on him his entire carriage changed remarkably. He carried his neck and tail arched and his stride became springier. And not only that, in the next few months he became the leader in the herd of colts.

Gently sliding down the strands of tail hair will relax and calm your horse.

When a horse's posture changes, his behavior changes too. By clamping his tail against his hindquarters, it became extremely tight and the colt was nervous of anything coming up behind him. When he changed his tail carriage, he relaxed his hindquarters and gained confidence.

It's fascinating to have someone do the Tail TTouches while you sit on your horse, bareback or with a saddle. You can feel the effects of the Tail TTouch through the horse's whole body; when you close your eyes, you can feel the movement of his entire spine. It's a good experience for horse and rider.

"Can we practice **Back Lifts** with Casamira?" asks Mandy.

Back Lifts are especially useful for a nervous horse who carries his head up high. Often his back is tight and dropped down, looking hollow-shaped. He needs to learn to relax the back and raise it so he can lengthen the neck and lower the head. Casamira doesn't have these problems, but the Back Lifts will still be beneficial for her to develop the elasticity useful for smooth gaits. I help Allison to do the Back Lift for the first time. We stand on each side of the young mare.

"First we just stroke Casamira's belly with our flat hands and do some Lying Leopard TTouches, so she can get used to someone touching her here."

Casamira stands quietly since she isn't ticklish.

"You start about three hand's widths behind the horse's front legs, on the midline of the belly, with your palms up and fingers curved together for more strength. Now press and release in a quick upward motion with your fingertips into the belly. This will cause Casamira to tighten her stomach muscles and raise her back. You don't actually lift the horse, you signal her to lift her back. If a horse doesn't respond to the pressure of your fingertips you can carefully use your fingernails, too. Once Casamira has learned to lift her back, you can change to an open-fingered, raking motion towards you and part way up the horse's barrel. For many horses this raking motion is enough to make them lift their backs, once they know what you want."

The children can see how Casamira's back comes up and lowers a little again.

"What's the difference between Back Lifts and Belly Lifts?" Claire

Linda's Tip

Tail TTouch with the rider on the horse's back

Doing the Tail TTouch creates a new feeling for both horse and rider. Try this: while you're doing the Tail TTouch on your horse have a friend sit on your horse with or without a saddle. When you are pulling the tail and then slowly releasing it, she'll be able to feel the horse's entire back moving; lengthening and shortening.

Claire prepares Casamira for some Back Lifts: she uses the Lying Leopard TTouch on Casamira's belly to get her used to being touched in this area.

Claire asks Casamira to tighten her abdominal muscles and lift her back.

At a glance

Back lifts

What are they? A TTouch that encourages a horse to raise his back by tightening his abdominal muscles.

Tools It is helpful to have medium-length fingernails.

What is it for? Horses who drop or hollow their backs away from the rider, are ewe-necked or swaybacked.

What does it do? By raising the back the horse can lower and relax his neck and relax his back muscles making him more comfortable.

Caution! Be sure to start this TTouch slowly. If you suddenly press your fingernails into your horse's belly it's understandable for him to kick at your hand. So don't punish him – take your time! If your horse is sensitive you may want to prepare him for Back Lifts by first doing some Clouded Leopard TTouches all over his belly, starting where the horse is most comfortable.

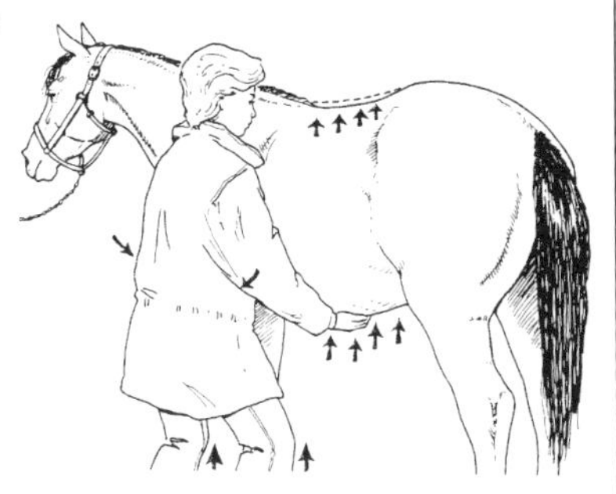

asks after practicing some Back Lifts.

"When you do Back Lifts, the horse uses the stomach muscles to raise the topline."

When you do **Belly Lifts** the horse relaxes his stomach muscles and breathes more deeply. It can be very helpful in cases of colic while waiting for the vet to arrive, and for stiff or "cold-backed" horses who don't like to be girthed or cinched up. It can also be a big help if your horse is

Belly Lifts with two people.

Belly Lifts with two people using a towel.

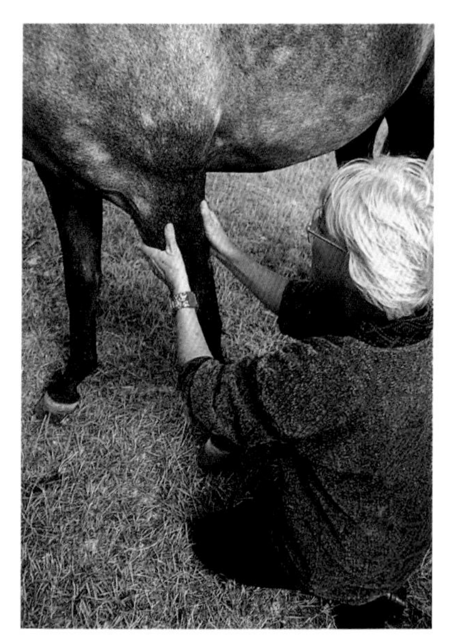
1 **The Octopus:** Put both hands on your horse's leg, starting about four inches below the elbow.

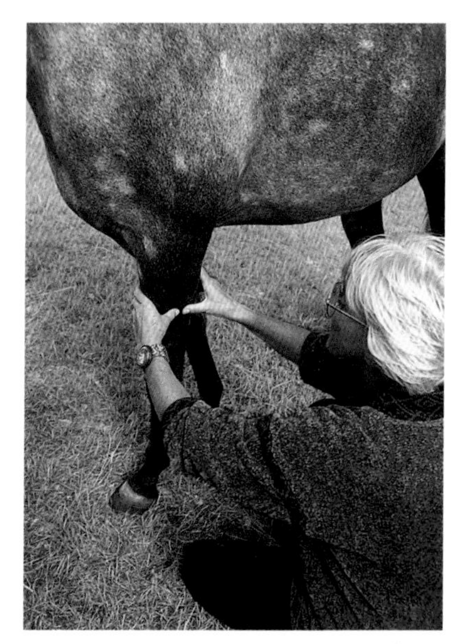
2 Now slide the thumbs down without pressure.

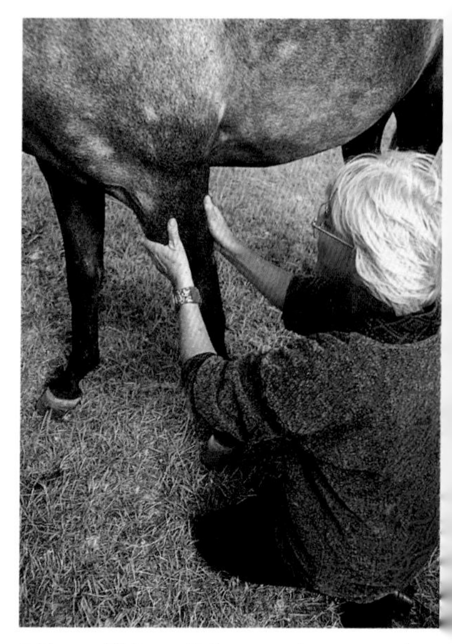
3 Use a lifting, sliding motion to push the skin upwards.

nervous. It is easiest to do Belly Lifts with two people, using either your flat hands or, better yet, a folded towel. You gently lift the belly and hold for ten to fifteen seconds. Then you very slowly release the pressure. You can start in the girth area and move back toward the flanks, six inches at a time.

We complete our session with Casamira by doing some leg work.

"There is a special TTouch I would like to show you," I tell the children after we have done some Python Lifts with Casamira. "I named this TTouch 'The Octopus' after an octopus I once worked on. Sometimes you feel like you need eight hands like the eight legs of an octopus to figure out this TTouch!"

The **Octopus TTouch** is very helpful for a horse who stumbles, shies or is nervous or spooky. Often such a horse doesn't know where he is putting his feet. When a horse is nervous or fearful his circulation may not be very good; the signals from his brain may be partially blocked so he doesn't feel his feet as well as he should. The Octopus TTouch increases the feeling and circulation in his legs.

You can imagine these signals to the brain moving like cars on a road. When the horse tenses, it's like a traffic jam on the highway – the signals, like traffic, may not get through. The flow of information between the leg and the brain is limited, which may cause the horse to stumble or shy because he is uncoordinated or feels unsafe. When you do the Octopus TTouch you increase the circulation and the "highways" open up again. With this TTouch the horse will feel his legs in a new way and improve his connection to the ground.

I'll show you how to do the Octopus step-by-step. It sounds more complicated than it really is. When you understand each step and have practiced it you can do the entire Octopus in one flowing movement.

- Start the Octopus TTouch about four inches below the horse's elbow. Place both hands around the leg, the fingers on the inside of the leg, the thumbs pointing straight up (see photo 1).
- Slide your thumbs down until the tips of the thumbs point toward each other (photo 2).
- Slide your thumbs lightly over the skin up and out to the side again (photo 3) and around to the inside of the leg (photo 4).
- Here your wrists cross and the backs of your hands turn slightly toward the inside of the leg. The

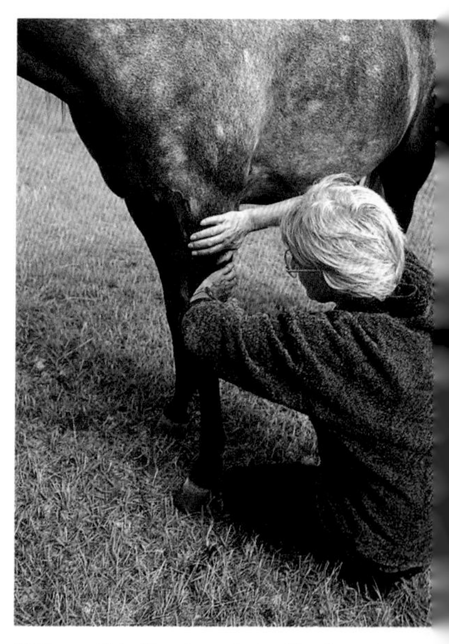
7 Now slide the hands to the front one on top of the other.

The hands slide to the inside of the
›g and cross there at the wrists.

5 The crossed hands slide down while you pull them slightly towards you.

6 The crossed hands slide back up on the inside of the leg.

Cross your hands at the wrists, put
›ur hands around the horse's leg and
ide down.

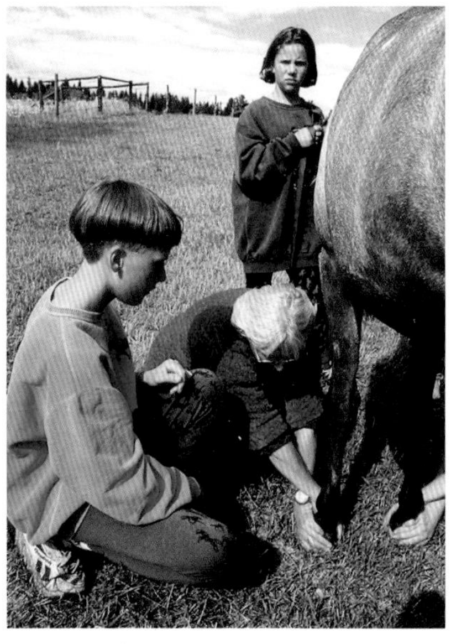

9 At the completion of each Octopus movement, put a little pressure on the toe and the heel of the hoof and pause for a few seconds.

rists lay one above the other as
ou continue the slide down the
›g, pulling slightly toward you.
The movement down should be
vice as far as the previous
novement up. So if you have
ushed the skin up for eight
nches on the outside of the leg,
ide your crossed wrists down
bout sixteen inches on the inside of the leg (see arrow on photo 5).

• Rest your hands where they are for a moment and take a breath.

• Now move the crossed hands back up the leg up again, to the same place where you first crossed them (photo 6)…

• …and slide your hands back to the outside of the leg. Here the right hand slides parallel above the left on the outside of the horse's leg. The thumb of the right hand should be about an inch above the little finger of the left hand, the palms are turned towards the horse (photo 7).

• Your hands now wrap around the leg again with the arms crossed. The thumbs point down and the fingers point toward each other on the inside of the leg (photo 8).

• Your hands slide down the horse's leg, all the way to the hoof. It's important not to stop at the fetlock joint, but to go all the way down to the ground with your hands. When you reach the ground, hold the toe and the heel of the hoof with a little pressure for a few moments to emphasize the connection to the ground. Your thumbs will be touching the ground (photo 9).

• Now you start the Octopus again, each time about five inches lower. You'll need about four Octopus TTouches for the entire leg. The last TTouch starts a little above the fetlock joint.

Casamira stands quietly and

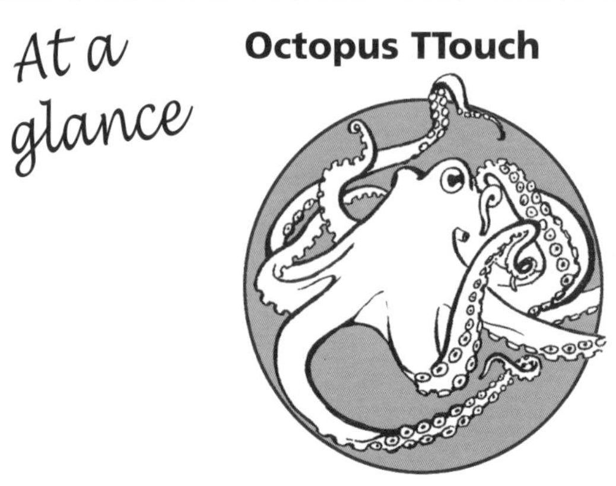

At a glance

Octopus TTouch

What is it?
A complicated series of movements on a horse's leg. The movements remind me of the arm movements of an octopus I once worked with in an aquarium. Usually an octopus is afraid of humans, and when stressed his skin turns dark red. The octopus I worked with learned through the TTouch that he did not need to be afraid of humans and stayed his normal color.

What is it for?
To improve your horse's gait and coordination. It's useful for horses who are nervous, shy or stumble by giving them more feeling in their legs.

What does it do?
With the help of the Octopus TTouch your horse can move with more awareness and less tension as well as lengthen his stride, which will become more even. His gait will improve and he'll be able to judge his footing or a jump more accurately.

Caution!
To be safer squat down next to your horse for this TTouch, but do not kneel! Stay to the side of your horse to avoid getting bumped by his knee if he suddenly brings his leg forward.

A well-earned break in the shady meadow in front of Robyn's house. I am telling stories of my experiences with horses all around the world, answering questions and showing Allison how the TTouch feels on her own body.

enjoys the Octopus TTouch. I'm showing it to a very attentive Geoff.

"It takes a little time to learn the Octopus, but once you know how to do it, it'll be a lot of fun." We also practice the Octopus TTouch on each other.

"I like trying the TTouch out with someone else," says Talia. "Then I know how the Octopus feels on my leg."

"Exactly! But that's not all. Tomorrow we'll try something fun without the horses."

"What is it?" everybody wants to know.

"Wait and see," is my answer, teasing them.

It's time to finish the session with Casamira. We bring her back to the barn, thank her and Mrs Goertz, and say good-bye.

Linda's Tip

Squatting down

Don't kneel down to clean your horse's hooves, bandage a leg or do leg TTouches. It's much safer to stay on your feet and squat down. It's important to be able to get up and away quickly in case your horse spooks or shies.

'he drive to the Aspengrove :questrian Academy is quite an xperience. The small road teadily winds its way uphill, first hrough the forest, then alongside astures with knee-high grass and himmering groves of aspen trees rowing up the mountain slope. Vhen we finally arrive at the table, we enjoy the breathtaking iew from the top of the hill. Iilda and Ron Wohlford greet us varmly and show us their exciting acility.

Aspengrove is one of the best iding schools I know. I wish all chool horses had such a good life: ach horse has his own open helter with a generous paddock, o he can eat in peace and get his wn, special diet. When the horses re not working, they are turned ut together to graze in a big herd n the vast mountainside pastures ear the riding school. There, they an run to their heart's content, lay together and scratch each ther. A real paradise for horses!

The tack room is perfectly rganized and tidy, bridles and addles in neat rows. From the iding arena you have an eagle's-ye view over rolling meadows, voods and faraway mountains.

"Do you need some horses right way?" Ron asks.

"Not yet!"

I see Geoff's disappointed face nd add: "First, we will have the urprise I mentioned yesterday: to ractice leading and learn how the orse feels, we are going to take ırns playing at being the horse!"

"But, Linda!" Geoff is skeptical, we all know how to lead a horse rith our eyes closed. What more there to learn?"

"Of course, I know you are all ble to lead your horses. You've shown me that. But today you'll learn to use a chain lead line and the wand to communicate clearly and without a struggle. I often see a horse almost dragging his handler along. When she counteracts and pushes her elbow into the horse's neck to bend his head towards her while trying to slow him down, it is not far from becoming a wrestling match."

"And it doesn't matter if a horse is small or big, it's always stronger!" says Mandy.

"That's true! Even an adult can have a hard time leading a Shetland pony who is fighting her and trying to get away. That's why the lead line with a chain is especially important for children. You can give light signals and still have more control if your horse pulls, shies or suddenly jumps to the side. The chain lead line is a very fine tool and at the same time a kind of emergency brake. With

Every horse has its own open stall with a spacious paddock. The horses can talk to each other over the fence, and eat and rest without being disturbed.

The horses in Aspengrove are lucky, they are well kept and lovingly cared for.

Angie says

Imagine being locked up in a small, dimly lit and stifling closet all by yourself, no friends, no frolicking around. Sounds like a prison, doesn't it? Unfortunately many horses spend the greater part of their lives in stalls or stables like this. Is it surprising that some horses become nervous, skittish and aggressive under these conditions? I am not surprised! Please keep in mind that horses are herd animals who need movement as a normal part of their lives. Horses need friends, light, fresh air and the chance to gallop around.

"Hold the chain between your thumb and forefinger to be able to give your 'human horse' light signals with a small movement of your wrist."

because they've seen people punish their horses roughly with it. We don't punish with the chain and don't use it alone, but only in combination with the wand and voice commands. We train the horse to respond to light signals instead of fighting with him. In my opinion, a horse can only be considered well trained when he can be led without any problems. I expect a well-trained horse to

"If you make a fist, you can't give light signals. Open your hand a little and make sure to keep your finger joints soft and flexible."

"Come on, horse! Aaand waaalk!" "Human horse" Claire willingly responds to my clear signal in the leading position Elegant Elephant.

"Not like this!" "Horse" Mandy knows how to defend herself! She kicks and shows clearly in horse language that sh doesn't like Geoff's signals.

TTEAM you can teach the horse to cooperate without getting in a wrestling match."

"I've heard that you shouldn't use a lead line with a chain. If I can't control my horse with a lead rope and halter why not use a bridle?" asks Geoff.

"Even with a bridle you may be tempted to pull and lean against your horse. Pulling on the bit hardens the horse's mouth and you may still not be able to control him. Let me show you how to communicate using light signals with a chain lead line and the wand. I know that many people are against the use of a chain,

"Aaand trot!" Claire is already practicing lungeing. Her playful "horse" jumps around and even tries to run off.

"No more!" I come to help Claire. "Be patient! "Encourage your 'horse' instead of punishing her. Then she'll want to work with you again."

ave good manners on the ground s well as under saddle. A horse vho is obedient on the ground vill usually be cooperative under addle. I often have difficult and ometimes even dangerous horses n my clinics whose owners can arely control them with a lead ope or a bridle while leading. In nany cases, these horses are also ifficult under saddle. After vorking with the chain lead line, vand and ground obstacles their ehavior changes surprisingly ast. They learn to become bedient and cooperate ttentively, to respond to light ignals and to respect humans. 'he best way to learn to use the hain and the wand is to practice vith each other."

The "human horse" intertwines er fingers and we make a figure ight with the chain around both ands and fasten the snap. I show ne children how to hold the chain ead line:

"The thumb nd forefinger old the chain. 'he nylon lead art is held in such way, so it does not wrap round your hand. Please don't ever wrap it around your hand! You need to be able to let go should your horse make a sudden jump. Even adults have been pulled over and dragged by horses while leading. Do you remember what you should **not** do with the chain?"

"Don't ever jerk on it!" says Mandy.

"Don't tie your horse with it!" adds Allison.

"Don't punish the horse with the chain!" exclaims Shanti.

"Good! Now you can go and try everything with your partners. See what it feels like when you jerk or pull on the lead line. How would you like it if you were a horse? Use your wand to give both clear signals and confusing signals. The 'horses' are allowed to defend themselves when they don't like something: they can kick, bite and try to run away. Just pretending, of course! Imagine how a horse would feel and try to 'walk in his hooves' for a bit."

Within a few minutes unruly "horses" are running past me and pairs are jumping over fences. Some are practicing small movements with great concentration.

ɔgether we are bringing in the horses from the big, rolling pastures in spengrove.

Angie says

Some horses are very spirited and just want to play and let off steam. They may not be able to focus on calm work right away, especially if they've been cooped up in a box stall. Don't take it personally if a horse is hard to control and nervous under saddle. Even a little bucking can be considered normal under these circumstances. Maybe you know how it feels when you cannot sit still in school any more and just need to get out and play like the kids in the photo below? Please give your horses the opportunity to play with each other and get rid of their extra energy. If you can't turn them loose to play do some TTouches or groundwork with them. Then they'll be able to be calm and attentive under saddle.

"This is really fun!" exclaims Geoff with sparkling eyes.

"I didn't realise that as a 'horse' you can really feel the slightest movement of the chain!" says Talia.

After a while everyone switches roles. Whoever has been a handler so far, now gets to be a "horse" and the "horses" become the handlers.

"I wonder how this would be if it were real?" Shanti says.

An interesting question!

We take a little break and then go with Ron to the big pasture to get some horses so we can practice the ground exercises.

First I demonstrate how to attach the chain to the halter. The halter needs to fit just right. The noseband should be about four inches under the cheekbone. The chin piece should fit so the halter doesn't slide when you lead the horse. Halters with round side rings work best. If they are square the chain gets stuck and can't slide.

If you feel unsure about using a chain, or have a young or very sensitive horse, you can use a lead line with a soft rope in place of the chain. This lead is attached in the same way as the chain and has a nylon endpiece, too. I call it the Zephyr lead. Foals should always be led with a Zephyr lead, as a chain is too heavy and severe in its effect. Remember, the chain and the wand are training tools. A well-trained horse can, of course, be led with a regular lead rope. I know horses who even do the ground exercises without a halter.

At a glance

Chain lead line

What is it? A six-foot soft nylon lead with a thirty-inch chain sewn on to it. We attach the chain to the halter so the chain crosses over the noseband of the halter or up the side.

Tools: I recommend using gloves to protect your hands.

What is it for? For the TTeam ground exercises and for controlling high-strung horses. You can lead a horse with this lead line without using force. It will encourage your horse to lower his head, helping him to overcome the flight instinct.

What does it do? It allows you to give clear signals so the horse learns to stop and slow down. Later, when you are riding he will respond to the same light signal from the reins.

Caution! Do not tie your horse with a chain lead line! If he pulls back he could injure his nose.When you lead your horse, only use short tug-and-release signals. The chain lead line is a wonderful tool when used properly. I only use it in combination with the wand, voice commands and my own body language. Don't use it to punish your horse! Keep your finger out of the metal triangle on the chain or the halter ring. Practice holding the end of the nylon lead in loops like "rabbit ears" (see photo 2 below) until it becomes second nature, then you won't accidentally wrap it around your hand.

1 "Pretend the snap is a dolphin that dives in the side ring and down."

2 "Cross the chain over the noseband and pull it from the inside to the outside through the ring on the other side of the halter."

3 "Now hook the snap in the upper ring on the side of the halter with the snap facing to the outside."

Naturally, their owners practiced with them until they knew the obstacles and would willingly follow voice commands and hand signals. They walk completely free next to their handlers – over a teeter-totter (see-saw), through the Labyrinth, through the zigzagged poles and the Star, through thick and thin! It is a wonderful feeling to have reached this level of communication and cooperation with your horse.

With TTEAM we teach horses to lead from both sides. This improves the coordination of both horses and humans. Think about it. We bridle and saddle our horses from the left. We lead them from the left and we mount from the left. Is it surprising that most horses bend better to the left than to the right? In Iceland it's different. There they are saddled and mounted from the right. You can help your horse to bend equally well to both sides by leading him through the ground exercises from the right side also.

On a small horse the chain may be too long. You can shorten it by taking the end through the highest ring of the halter and attaching it back to itself. Doubling the chain on one side will shorten it on the other side.

There are several ways to attach the chain to the halter. Over the nose for horses who are difficult to control, or up the side, when you want to lower your horse's head. To lower the head, thread the chain through the lower ring, up through the top ring and then attach it back to itself as shown in the photo. I have found that horses learn to lower their heads when the chain is used in this fashion.

"Why is it so important to have a horse's head low?" asks Claire.

"A good question! Horses are flighty by nature. That means they

The Zephyr lead is especially suitable for working with very sensitive horses or foals. Attach it in the same way as the chain.

flee as soon as they feel threatened. This is called the flight reflex. The horse does not think about this behavior, he simply runs away by instinct, unless he is trained otherwise. Probably you've noticed that horses throw up their head when they are frightened. Their entire body is on alert and they're ready to race off at the slightest sound. This is why it's so important for horses to lower their heads. As soon as the head is lowered the flight reflex is no longer activated. The horse calms down; he is able to think."

"Think? Can horses really think?" Geoff wants to know.

"Many people assume that humans are the only beings on the planet who are able to think. That's not so! Horses are able to think and I'm convinced that they become more intelligent through TTEAM work."

A horse who reacts or is controlled by reflexes isn't thinking, he's only acting from his deep-seated instincts. When he learns to think, he can evaluate a situation and overcome the flight instinct. He can look at something that scared him and realize that it isn't dangerous. He can relax and doesn't need to run away. A safe riding horse needs to learn self-control.

When a horse is tense and high-headed he can't think. So, it's important that the handler asks the horse to lower his head when he is nervous. It's useful for doing ground exercises, so he can see where he is stepping and also helps him to stay calm and relaxed.

"Should the head always be as

You can shorten a chain that is too long like this: thread it through the upper ring on the side of the halter and close the snap on the side.

You can attach the chain on the side only. This works like magic to lower a horse's head.

low as possible?" asks Claire.

"Not always. It depends on the horse. If a horse is lazy or slow, bring his head up. Then he'll be better balanced and you'll be able to speed him up. When a nervous horse with high head carriage and tight back and neck learns to lower his head, his performance will improve no matter what you are asking him to do – pleasure riding, dressage, jumping, driving or Western riding."

Now the children are ready to try out what they have learned with the horses.

"How did you first think of doing these ground exercises?" asks Talia as we enter the riding arena.

"I was one year younger than you are now. You know I started training horses as a young girl. But very differently! I didn't know any better and had to use the old-fashioned method. Young horses were chased in a round pen until they got tired and stopped bucking. But many still bucked every once in a while when they graduated from the round pen. I can't count how many times I was bucked off from young horses trained in this way. One evening as I was riding home from Briarcrest an old man with a cane hobbled down his driveway and stopped me. He said he had watched me ride by every day for many months and wanted to give me a special book. This book described how to start a young horse under saddle, first preparing him by driving him from the ground, so he would not be afraid. This book was a revelation for me. I read it from cover to cover and was eager to try out this method. The opportunity came soon, when a friend of my parents asked me to start her Thoroughbred mare under saddle. I followed the book step by step, putting a light saddle on her and driving her from the ground by threading two lunge lines through the stirrups and hooking them to the snaffle rings. When I mounted her for the first time a week later, I was a happy camper. She was calm and obedient, didn't buck and seemed to enjoy the experience. This was the relationship with a young horse I had always dreamed of."

"In the following years I developed methods of ground driving which were safe for the most inexperienced amateur. I devised new ground exercises which instilled confidence and balance in horses and deepened their relationships with their riders. I discovered that ground work was not just useful for starting young horses; most horse and even humans can learn much from this work. Top horses of all disciplines have improved their performance through ground exercises. Horses that run away and horses with all kinds of difficulties have been able to lear new behavior. Ground exercises prepare a horse to respond to ligh signals when being ridden. Slow, stubborn or so-called lazy horses develop more ambition and learn to cooperate willingly. High-

At a glance

TTEAM tools

1. Zephyr lead A soft rope lead line that is attached across the noseband of the halter in the same way as the chain lead line.

2. Groomas and Loopa glove Grooming brushes and a mitt with soft rounded rubber pimples.

3. Neck ring A ring made from a stiff rope that can be adjusted for size.

4. Balance rein A seven-foot long, half-inch wide rope around the horse's neck as an additional rein.

5. Wand A four-foot, stiff whip, preferably white with a hard plastic "button" on the end. I sometimes call it my "magic wand" because you can do so many wonderful things with it.

6. Body wrap Made from two elastic bandages, six feet long and four inches wide.

7.Chain lead line A thirty-inch chain attached to a six-foot nylon lead line. (It should not be shorter, for safety reasons.)

trung horses calm down and
earn to go forward from the
ider's signal, instead of storming
head out of tension or fear. It's a
;reat tool for deepening the bond
vith your horse."

Ve've arrived in the riding arena.
take the gray gelding Drummer
3oy to demonstrate the leading
osition **Elegant Elephant:**

When leading from the left take
he end of the lead line and the
vand in your left hand. Stay
orward by the horse's head,
ather than back by the shoulder.
Hold the wand in the middle, with
he "button" end chest-high, about
wo and a half feet in front of your horse's head. With the right hand hold the chain about six inches from the halter. With a tall or nervous horse you may want to slide your hand further away from the halter to give the horse some slack.

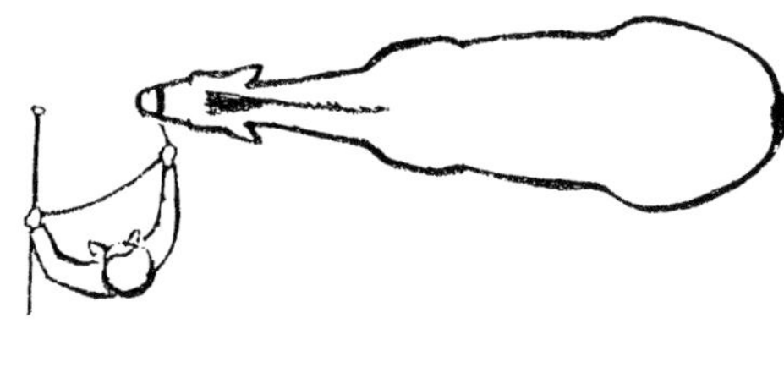

This is the leading position Elegant Elephant. You show the horse the way with the wand.

- As you move forward, use the wand like a long arm to indicate with the "button" end which direction you want your horse to go in. Imagine that the horse's nose has changed into an elephant's trunk and is following the wand. At the same time, give a clear voice command and a gentle signal on the chain to go forward. It is important not to pull on the chain, but only give a light signal and then release. The horse should

At a glance

Elegant Elephant

What is it?

This is the strongest leading position and gives you the most control over your horse. I have named this leading position the Elegant Elephant in honor of the elephant Empress in the Honolulu Zoo. I imagine the horse having an elephant's trunk and following the forward motion of the wand with it.

What is it for?

It is especially useful for leading young horses, or for horses who have too much energy.

What does it do?

The horse learns to respect you and to respond to your signals. You can lead your horse safely and control him without force. He learns self-control and moves in balance.

Caution!

It is dangerous to hook your finger in the metal triangle of the chain or the side ring of the halter! Practice holding the lead line in "rabbit ears" (see photos page 42) until it becomes second nature to make sure you won't wrap it around your hand by accident.

Mandy holds the end of the chain in her right hand and the nylon lead in her left.

start walking on the release, not on the pull.

• To stop, stay even with his head, not at his shoulder. Give the voice command "Whoa" and draw out the sound as you are breathing out: "Whooooooa". Hold the tone until your horse stops. This also encourages you to breathe deeply. At the same time, move the wand once or twice with a soft movement of your wrist, keep the tip about two and half feet in front of your horse's head in the area between his eyes and nose. Make it a calm motion, not a wild commotion. Tap the horse's chest once or twice while you give him a signal to stop with the chain – a light tug backward and release. Now, when he's still, you can stroke your horse on the neck with the wand and praise him.

I spend a few minutes showing the children the Elegant Elephant. Drummer Boy turns out to be fast learner. He quickly understands my signals and follows them willingly. I praise him lavishly and turn him over to Talia. "It's your turn!"

In the beginning it's not easy to remember all the many details of the leading positions. Like most riding students, Talia has learned to walk at her horse's shoulder. She keeps drifting back to the shoulder rather than staying up at Drummer Boy's head. She pulls his head toward her and can't stop him on a straight line.

I show Talia where she needs to stand to avoid pulling Drummer Boy's head around to her.

"It's much safer to stand at his head. Suppose Drummer Boy suddenly jumped in your direction! When you are leading from the shoulder you can get knocked down or stepped on. By leading him at the head, the horse can see you and the wand, and you have a better chance of controlling him."

"But I'm used to leading back at the shoulder!"

"I know! But how about practicing up by the head and seeing how you feel about it?"

After a few more tries Talia begins to get the idea and Drummer Boy cooperates willingly. I'm proud of both of them.

"Now I'll show you another way to lead a horse."

I demonstrate the **Dingo** leading position with Cody. This position will calm a nervous horse, wake up a lazy one and retrain a stubborn one. The name was inspired by the wild dog that lives in Australia. When you stroke the back think of "ding" and when you tap the croup it's "go forward" as in Ding-go.

When you do the Dingo, you hold the lead line so there is a loo on either side of the hand, rather than around it. The loops look lik big "rabbit ears" (see photos 2 an 3 on page 42). Hold the chain a few inches away from the halter between the thumb and forefinge of the left hand. The right hand holds the wand. The Dingo consists of four steps:

1. Get your horse's attention with a light signal from the chain, which prepares him to move. Ideally you want him to flex at hi poll.

2. Stroke the back two or three times with the wand from the

At a glance

Dingo

What is it? A leading position that I've named after the wild dog found in Australia.

What is it for? To teach a horse to come forward from a signal on the chain with one hand and the other hand stroking the wand twice on his back and tapping him three times on the croup. This is how I teach horses to lead, or retrain horses who pull back when tied. Later, this tapping on the croup can be used under saddle on horses who are lazy o slow.

What does it do? It teaches a horse to lead obediently from pressure on the head alone. It's also an extremely good exercise for teaching a horse to load into a trailer.

Caution! It is important to prepare your horse for the tap of the wand on his croup by stroking along his back several times, so you don't startle him.

vithers to the croup. Your horse houldn't move forward yet, but imply become more aware of his ack from the stroking.

3. Give a light signal forward vith the chain…

4. …and tap the croup three mes using a small circular, orward motion with the tip of the vand.

In the beginning you can also ive a voice command: "Aaaaand vaaaalk" in the third step as you ive the horse a light signal on the hain to go forward.

This is a good position for eading a horse a short way. When ou lead him a longer distance ou should change the position to e Dolphin Flickering Through e Waves (see pages 49-50) or the race of the Cheetah (see pages 0-51).

o stop a horse from the Dingo ou can use the leading position

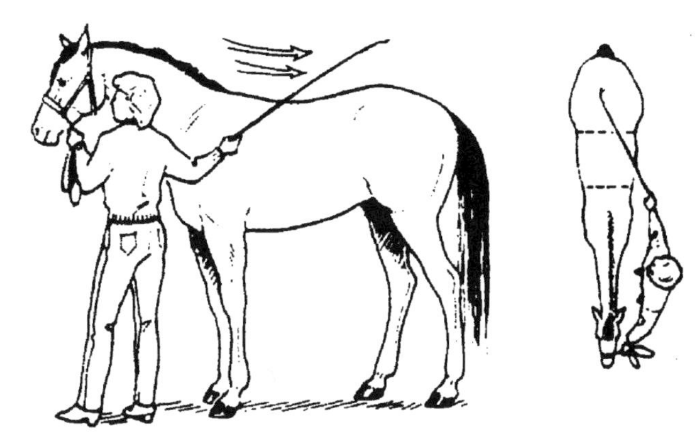

In the Dingo you stroke the horse's back two times with the wand.

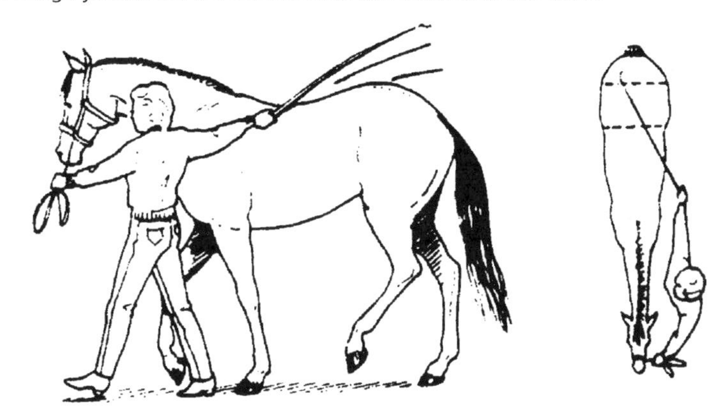

You tap the horse three times lightly on the croup.

ove: The children stroke the horse's ack with their wands.

ove right: The horses are stopped in e leading position Cuing the Camel ee overleaf), by tapping their chests.

e Dingo at a walk: the children are alking next to their horses with their rsos slightly turned.

At a glance

Cuing the Camel

What is it?

A leading position to stop a horse by tapping him on the chest with the wand. In Australia I've ridden and worked with camels on safari. When combined with the Dingo, this leading position reminds me of the three complicated stages it takes for a camel to lie down.

What is it for?

To teach your horse to shift his center of gravity back and come to a stop in balance.

What does it do?

Your horse learns to stop from the combination of the chain pressure and the light taps on the chest without throwing his head up or bringing his head too close to his chest. You can also use the same signal when riding without a bridle. (See Mandy stopping Cody on page 99.)

Caution!

Keep your hand about four inches away from the halter on the chain to keep your horse straight. Make sure you don't pull his head to the side and put him off balance.

Cuing the Camel. From the Dingo, bring the wand away from the croup and along the side of the horse to the front of the chest. Signal your horse to stop by giving the voice command "Whoooa" as you give a light signal with the chain and a tap on the chest to stop.

There's another way to stop your horse from the Dingo, using **Boomer's Bound**.

Boomer's Bound.

To give a signal to stop bring the wand over the horse's head in a smooth motion about two feet in front of the head. At the same time give a voice command "Whoa" and a signal with the chain to stop.

These different leading positions demand a good deal of concentration. Sometimes you hold the lead line in the left hand, sometimes in the right. You're walking forwards, but your torso is turned sideways. The wand is also used in many different and new ways. That's why it's helpful to practice the leading positions first without a horse. You'll find as your coordination improves from the ground exercises, so will your riding.

Geoff has a problem with the pinto gelding, Gordi. He won't go forward, even though Geoff is giving all the right signals.

"Just a little tapping isn't enough for him," Geoff complains. "He's standing there like he has roots."

"I know how you feel! Many years before the TTouch I remember a Haflinger mare who

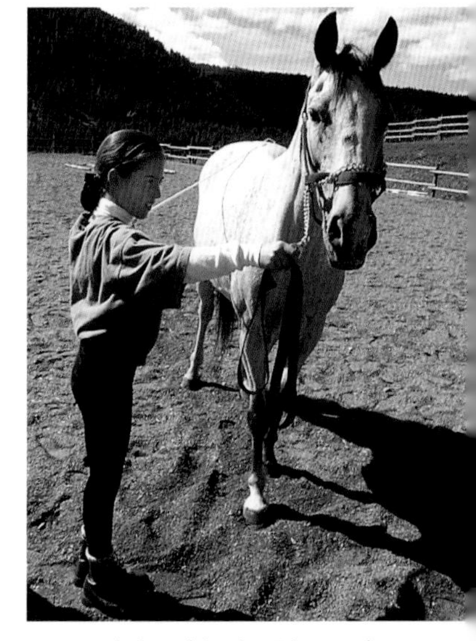

Forward signal in the Dingo: the hindquarters are activated with the wand.

Stopping from the Dingo: Allison uses the leading position Cuing the Camel.

efused to go forward like Gordi. I apped her croup a few times, but t didn't help. All she did was ighten her hindquarters. Finally I ;ave her a whack, and she bucked nd jumped forward. I suddenly nderstood: this mare had never earned to go forward from a tap n the croup. She wasn't very ware of her body, either, and she vasn't really connected through er back. I had to teach her from cratch to go forward from a tap. Nowadays, I would do TTouches n her and teach her to go forward vith the Dingo instead of vhacking her. I have learned so nuch since that time. That mare vasn't just stubborn, as her wners had suspected, and certainly didn't deserve to be punished. She simply didn't understand what we wanted her to do."

"Do you think Gordi has the same problem?" Geoff asks hesitantly.

"Probably. In any case, it's always better to give a little thought to what might be causing a problem, rather than just hitting a horse."

Geoff and I do some Lick of the Cow's Tongue TTouches with Gordi. Then I stroke his entire body with the wand.

"Now try it again. Give him a clear signal with the chain and tap him on the croup. Support the command with your voice and a forward motion of your body."

Gordi immediately steps forward! Geoff is very happy and Gordi seems to be content.

"Linda!" Shanti shrugs her shoulders in frustration, "Erin is always crowding me. How can I teach him to keep his distance?"

"It's not comfortable to have a horse crowd you, especially if you're small and the horse is big."

"You're right," Shanti sighs and turns Erin over to me.

"This is an opportunity to use a leading position I call **Dolphin Flickering Through the Waves**. You start with the Dingo. As your horse steps forward, slide your hand further away on the lead line. Then give your horse a flick on top of the croup with the tip of the wand, next on the shoulder, then a light tap on the top of the neck and finish with a soft flick on the side of the nose as if you were using a paint brush. Tapping your horse lightly on these four points

We touch these four points with the wand for the Dolphin Flickering Through the Waves.

with the wand will keep him moving in a straight line about four feet from you. It's good to start this exercise walking in a straight line and then graduate to a semicircle. These are the preparatory steps for lungeing."

"And how do I stop?" asks Shanti, who has followed each of my movements attentively.

"To stop, you change to the

At a glance

Boomer's Bound

What is it? Another leading position to stop your horse after starting him from the Dingo leading position, by moving the wand smoothly over the neck and the ears and moving it in front of the face to stop the horse. The big bounding kangaroos in Australia, known as "Boomers", inspired this name.

What is it for? Especially helpful for horses who are afraid of anything moving above their neck and head. Because it encourages horses to lose their fear of things overhead, it is a good exercise to prepare a horse for loading.

What does it do? It can stop a horse from being head-shy. It is also useful for preparing a young horse to be mounted, so he won't be spooked when a rider gets on and is above him for the first time.

Caution! The movement with the wand above the head of your horse should be made slowly, so he isn't afraid.

Talia keeps her horse at a distance with the Dolphin at the withers.

At a glance

Dolphin Flickering Through the Waves

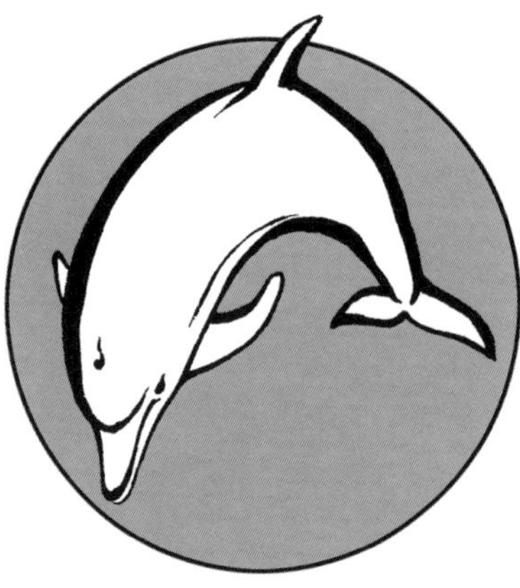

What is it?

A leading position I have named after my dolphin friend "Holey Fin". I met her while traveling on the west coast of Australia and visited her every day. During the next couple of years I thought of her often. When I returned to Australia to the beach where she lived, she came straight to me and touched my cheek softly with her nose. She had never done that before! I'm sure she recognized me. In this leading position, the tip of your wand jumps softly from point to point over the horse like a dolphin leaping through the waves, from the croup to the withers to the neck to the nose.

What is it for?

As a preparation for lungeing and for horses who crowd you and will not keep their distance. Also horses who are afraid to be touched or are head-shy.

What does it do?

The horse learns to move forward in a straight line at the pace you want and four feet away, keeping his distance from you. He learns to respond to signals from the wand without fear.

Caution!

It's important to keep the touch of the wand light and precise. Especially in the area of the head and neck, the touch of the wand should be as soft as the stroke of a brush.

leading position **Grace of the Cheetah**. You have to be as quick and as graceful as a cheetah to switch the wand from the right hand to the left hand and move it ahead of the horse's nose as you are walking. If your previous leading position was the Dolphin, you'll need to transfer the wand from the right hand to the left. You can do it like this: transfer the wand over to the left hand which is holding the end of the lead line and slide your right hand up the lead about thirty inches. To stop your horse make a short motion with the wand about three feet ahead of your horse and then tap him lightly on the chest as you say 'Whoa'."

Practice this while your horse is standing. It might be helpful to have someone hold the horse still.

To start your horse moving

You switch from the Dolphin...

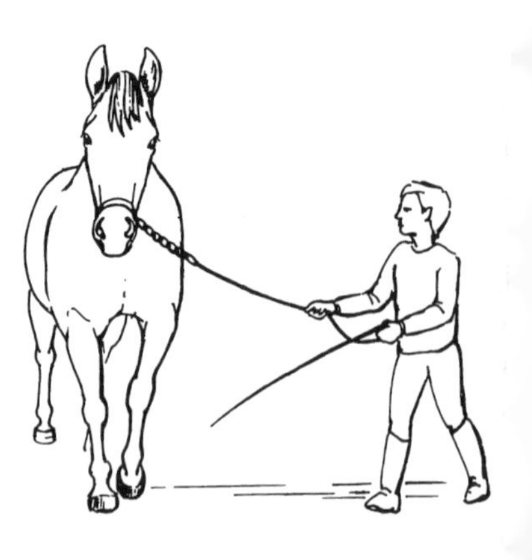

...to the Grace of the Cheetah

At a glance

Grace of the Cheetah

What is it? A leading position named for a cheetah. Her long tail made me think of the use of the wand. I remember two young cheetahs, Juba and Mojo, at the Fossil Rim Wildlife Center in Texas, who had been separated very early from their mother. Unfortunately they had become terrified of people. After I had worked on them with TTouches and the wand they became very friendly. They could even be led around just by following the tip of the wand.

What is it for? To each your horse to follow the movement of the wand several feet away from you and to stop from a signal from the wand combined with your voice.

What does it do? The horse learns to listen to your signals even when you are giving them from a distance. Insecure horses who like humans very close for reassurance become more confident.

Caution! You want your horse to stop without turning towards you so he learns to think, not just react. Do not apply too much pressure on his head or you can easily pull the horse around towards you.Tap lightly, don't poke him on the neck to keep your horse at a distance.

ɔrward from this position there re two different exercises:

(a) Show the horse the way with he tip of the wand, by touching im softly between the nostrils nd then pulling the wand ɔrward with a gliding motion. At he same time, give a forward ignal with the chain, and the erbal command "And Waaaaalk" nd start walking yourself. The orse will follow you naturally.

(b) Tap your horse's chest with circular motion and pull the vand forward with a gliding notion. Your horse will go forward in balance.

To stop him, use your voice and a tap of the wand on the chest. Move the wand up and down a few inches once or twice about three feet in front of his nose, using a flick of the wrist to signal with the wand. Keep the wand at the level of your horse's nose. Once he's stopped, stroke him on the chest with the wand to praise and reassure him.

Shanti takes her horse and practices Dolphin Flickering Through the Waves and Grace of the Cheetah herself. Erin tries to crowd once more, but a quick tap behind the ears keeps him away from her. I can tell how relieved Shanti is. She's been able to correct her horse with gentle means!

I'm observing Mandy, who is working with Cody. This gelding tends to throw his head up and tries to walk faster. Mandy has a hard time controlling him. I come to her rescue with a Zephyr lead (see pages 42 and 44) and the wand.

Linda's Tip

When your horse is crowding you

There are horses who tend to crowd you when you are leading them. This is not only unpleasant but actually dangerous. If your horse shies you don't have enough space to get out of his way. But how do you keep your horse at a safe distance?

- You can hold the chain lead line with your index finger and thumb about four inches away from the halter and then push your horse's head away from you.
- Or, you can hold the wand in the middle with the "button" end up and slowly move it like a windshield wiper between you and your horse. I call this exercise the Fanning Peacock because I visualize the movement of the wand like the tail of a peacock. You set a clear boundary your horse will learn to respect.

At a glance

Journey of the Homing Pigeon

What is it?
A leading position with two people, both with wands in the Grace of the Cheetah position, leading the horse. They lead from both sides like the open wings of a dove. I imagine that the horse will focus or "home in" on the wands like a homing pigeon.

Tools:
For this leading position you need one chain lead line, one Zephyr lead and two wands.

What is it for?
To teach the horse to overcome the flight instinct, to concentrate, become more balanced and cooperate more willingly. He also gets used to being led from both sides.

What does it do?
Both sides of the brain are activated. The horse needs to pay attention to the left and the right simultaneously. This enhances his ability to learn and teaches him to be cooperative.

Caution!
It is important to communicate clearly to your partner. It must be understood who will let go and who will stay with the horse should he suddenly balk, leap to the side or rear. In such a situation one person needs to let go while the other handles the horse. Be sure not to crowd your horse; have one handler be three feet away from the chain so the horse won't feel claustrophobic.

"Let's lead Cody in the **Homing Pigeon**," I suggest. "He'll learn to respond to light signals and control himself. Later, being ridden, he'll also be able to understand light signals."

The other children are watching as I attach the Zephyr lead on the other side of the halter so that it crosses the chain on top of the noseband.

"You take the lead," I say to Mandy.

When two people are leading a horse it's important to be clear from the beginning who will be in charge. Otherwise, one person will want to go left, the other one to the right, and the horse won't know what to do at all. We agree that I'll follow Mandy and that she'll tell me ahead of time where she wants to go. The person walking on the outside of a tight turn has to make bigger steps than the one leading on the inside, so the horse should slow down to make it easier. The Homing Pigeon requires cooperation between humans and horse. With practice, it's fun to work together. You learn to respect and take care of one another. It's TTEAM work in every sense of the word!

We can do the Homing Pigeon using various leading positions:

• Both handlers can use the wand and the chain as in the Grace of the Cheetah. To walk forward, the person in charge gives the signals with the chain, the wand and the voice. Both wands are held at the level of the nose to get the horse to concentrate on them. The wands are kept well out in front of the horse to show him the direction you want him to go in. Both handlers start walking at the same time.

To stop, the signals are given from one or from both persons,

The horse focuses on the two wands in front of his nose.

ɔove: "This is the horse's 'motor'. By ıpping here with a circular motion to ıe front you 'start the motor'."

ɒp right: Mandy gives forward signals the Dingo, while Talia stays in the race of the Cheetah.

ght: "Talia, it's better to shorten your ad a little in the Homing Pigeon, but ay in your leading position Grace of ıe Cheetah."

epending upon the horse.

• If your horse is too fast, the erson in control should switch to ıe Elegant Elephant to have more ɔntrol.

• When working with a slow ɔrse the person in command ıould switch to the Dingo ɔsition, while her partner stays rther away in the Grace of the heetah position.

landy's gelding Cody calms ɔwn in the Homing Pigeon. He laxes and follows our signals tentively. After a while, we vitch roles. Now I'm in charge ıd decide where we're going and landy follows along.

"We want to try this, too!" the hers exclaim.

We tie a few horses with lead pes attached to string on the nce posts (no chains, of course!) and work in pairs with the other horses.

"This is really fun!" Geoff says happily after he and Claire have succeeded at making a serpentine with their horse.

"How did you ever think of all the different names for the leading positions?" Allison wants to know as we're driving back to Aspengrove the following day.

"I was in Australia leading a group of people. We went riding on camels in the outback in the middle of the country, then went

Shanti uses the Elegant Elephant to slow down her horse.

looking for dolphins on the coast. Of course, I was giving some TTEAM clinics as well. The leading positions, back then, had quite boring numbers instead of names and it was difficult to remember them. Every morning, one of the women on our trip taught us T'ai Chi Chuan, a Chinese martial art. The movements had beautiful names, such as: Greeting the Sun or Arching the Bow. This inspired me to give my TTouches and leading positions names from the animal kingdom. A four-hour inland flight across the Australian continent gave us a great chance to think about names. 'No one leaves the plane until we have all the names!' I announced. Everyone laughed, but when the plane landed we had them all!"

"That's why you named one the Dingo and another Boomer's Bound," says Mandy.

"Yes, and with each TTouch or leading position I think about that particular animal. The animals need our help. I often have dream that they feel our thoughts

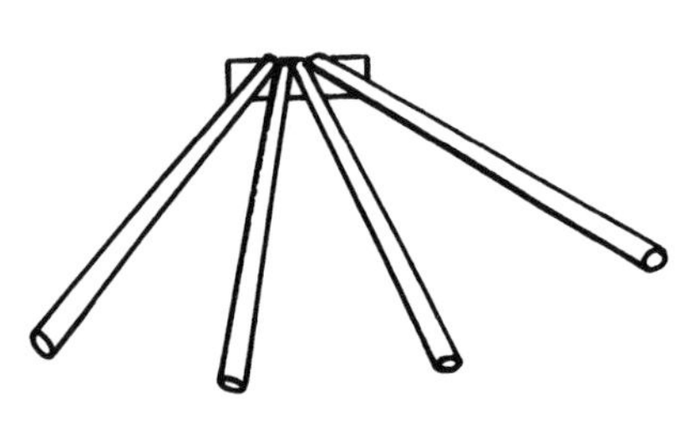

The Star

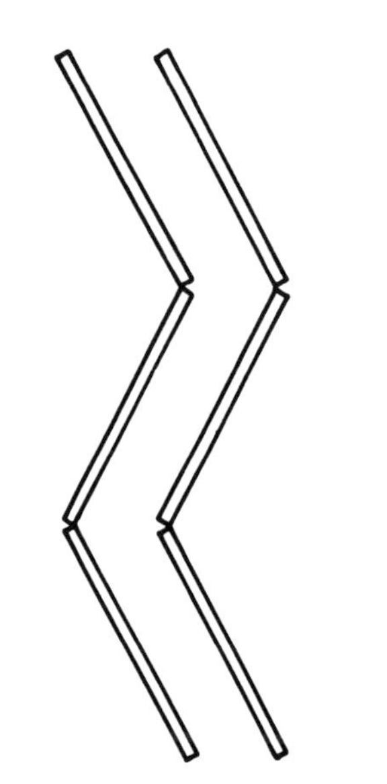

The Zigzag

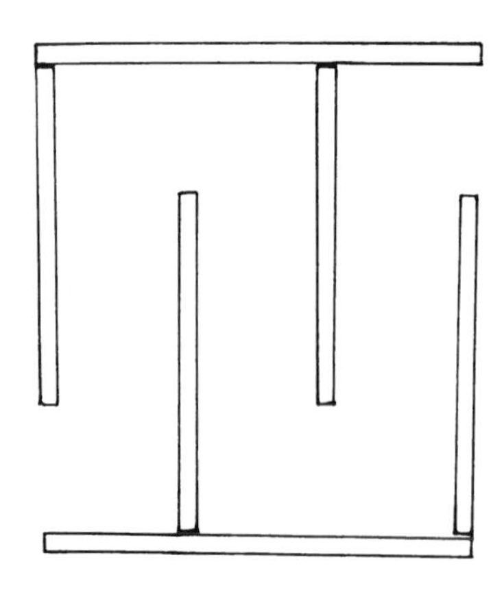

The Labyrinth

At a glance

Ground obstacles

What are they? I use many ground obstacles. Most of them are built from poles, barrels, tires, straw bales, hay bales and plastic. In this book we use the following obstacles: the Star, the teeter-totter (see-saw), the platform, the bridge and the Zigzag.

What is it for? For building confidence. To teach a horse to willingly cooperate and trust you. Working with ground obstacles improves balance and coordination in all horses, and is especially good for timid and fearful horses. This groundwork is also great basic training for young horses.

What does it do? The ground obstacles provide a positive challenge for your horse and improve his learning ability. He learns to think and place his feet carefully. He learns to listen to your signals precisely, to follow and trust you. It's also lots of fun!

Caution! It is important to work step-by-step and to prepare your horse slowly for difficult tasks. Also, use safe materials: make sure that the boards for a teeter-totter are strong enough and that there are no protruding nails in any of the poles.

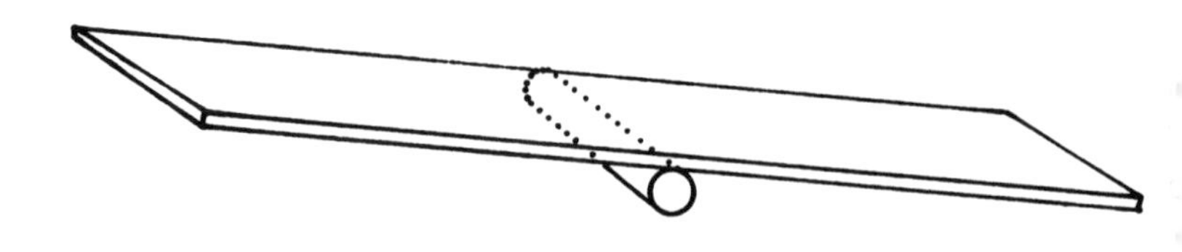

The teeter-totter (See-saw)

"Linda, my lead line is all tangled! Please show me again
ow you hold the looped end for the Elegant Elephant
osition.

2 "Don't be discouraged! All it takes is a little practice. I take the end of the lead line in a big loop in my left hand."

"When you hold the lead line like this you can't
:cidentally wrap it around your hand and you can make it
nger any time you want."

4 "If you open the hand more you will be able to give your horse light signals with the chain with a little movement of your wrist."

5 "I hold the chain between the thumb and the index finger. My hand is soft and not closed in a fist. Now I can have good control."

:aching out to them."

"What are we going to do
day?" Mandy wants to know.

"We'll work with ground
ɔstacles. That gives us a chance
practice all the leading positions
e learned yesterday."

We arrive in Aspengrove and get the horses from the paddocks below the riding arena where they rest and feed between lessons. Ron has already prepared some colorful jump poles and a box. We'll use them to build the Labyrinth and the Star in the riding arena.

"What can the horses learn from these ground obstacles?" is my question for the children.

"They learn to bend in the Labyrinth," Mandy answers.

"That's right. They learn to pay attention to where they put their feet. They learn balance and coordination and to follow you step-by-step. You can learn a lot, too. By switching from one leading position to the next, your balance and coordination will improve and you'll be surprised how it will affect your riding."

"And the Star?" asks Claire.

"The horse learns to bend as he lifts his legs and shortens or lengthens his stride."

The poles on the inside of the Star are raised higher than

1 Mandy stops Esprit in front of the pole and asks her to wait for a signal to come forward.

2 "Aaand walk!" Esprit follows Mandy willingly over the poles of the Labyrinth. She carefully picks up her feet and doesn't bump into the poles.

3 "Just a moment! It would be more effective to hold the wand lower. A small movement from your wrist can be a clear signal to stop."

4 "Very good, Mandy! Esprit understands your signal and stops. Your position at a right angle to the head makes it eas for her."

5 "Great! You have done really well. Make sure that your horse doesn't hurry over the poles at the end but moves forward steadily."

those outside. This is a very good exercise for horses who have a tendency to stumble. They become more sure-footed, their gait improves, their backs become more flexible and the shoulders have a greater range of motion.

The Labyrinth

"How many poles do you use for the Labyrinth?" Geoff wants to know.

"We need six poles, each about ten feet long."

"How far apart do they need to be?" asks Talia, already bringing the first pole.

"It depends on the size of your horse. If your horse is big, hasn't learned to bend very well yet, or isn't well balanced, put the poles further apart. If you have a small agile horse you can put the poles closer together. That makes for tighter turns and your horse need to bend more. In the beginning you can put the poles four feet apart."

Everyone is helping to carry the poles for the Labyrinth. Even Amadeus carries a pole with Shanti.

"Stop! We can't use this one!" I suddenly exclaim.

"But it is just as long as the others!" says Shanti.

"That's true, but look at this. 'here's a bolt sticking out of the ide. A horse could hurt himself 'ery easily on this!"

"Oh no, I didn't see that at all!" hanti is concerned.

"This bolt can easily be overlooked," I admit, "but that's why it's so important to carefully xamine all materials before you se them for ground obstacles." hanti exchanges the pole. Soon verything is ready and we go to et the horses.

Allison leads Cody, the chestnut elding, through the Labyrinth. he starts out in the leading osition Elegant Elephant. But her ifficulties begin in the first orner. Cody has stepped over to e left with his front legs, but ow he doesn't seem to know how o finish the curve and has topped.

"Switch to the Dingo," I suggest. Then you can show him that he eeds to engage his hindquarters o get around the corner. The indquarters are the horse's motor, and by using the Dingo ou activate his 'motor'. That's lso very important when riding. ' your horse has difficulty ending he can learn that in the abyrinth."

Allison switches to the Dingo nd Cody steps up and bends. In e next curve he needs to bend to e right. Allison switches to the legant Elephant again to show im the way.

'he Star

Linda!" Geoff calls me to the Star. We're stuck!"

Geoff has led his horse too close o the middle. Gordi is not used to icking up his feet so high.

"Start on the outside or just lay e poles on the ground," I uggest. "It's important not to

1 Shanti is using the Elegant Elephant and a Zephyr lead to walk Silver through the Labyrinth.

2 In the curve to the right she stays beautifully at the level of Silver's head and shows her the way around the corner with the wand.

3 They are already around the curve. Shanti and Silver are both concentrating and work together well.

4 Shanti stops the mare again with a light tap on the chest and praises her.

Linda's Tip

Making the work in the Star easier

If your horse has difficulties stepping over the higher poles in the middle of the Star and always hits them with his feet, you can make this exercise easier for him:

- Move the poles farther apart and lead your horse as far on the outside of the Star as possible. The poles are lower here and your horse won't need to bend as much.
- Stop your horse outside of the Star and tap each hoof for about thirty seconds with the 'button' of your wand to make him more aware of his hooves.
- For some horses you'll need to lay the poles flat on the ground to begin. Then raise one at a time.

1 Claire asks the chestnut gelding to come forward in the Elegant Elephant.

2 "Claire, it would be better if you were one more step ahead of your horse!"

overface your horse and make an exercise too difficult for him. Instead, make the task a little easier, so both of you will keep having fun."

This attitude is an important principle of the TTEAM work that I call "chunking". This means breaking a lesson into small steps that are easier to learn. If your horse has difficulties with the Star, for example, you can start out by just leading your horse over some poles on the ground. When this goes well, you can lay the poles with the ends together on one side, and fanned out on the other. This keeps the distances between the poles uneven. Your horse needs to make bigger steps on one side or the other. When your horse has accomplished this stage, raise the poles in the middle by propping them on a box. This way your horse will become more confident, because he knows he can do the things you are asking him to do. Of course, it's important to praise your horse every time he succeeds. Let him know that he has done well and you are happy with his accomplishments. But also remain friendly and understanding when he makes a mistake. Encourage him, and let both of you learn from his mistakes.

Geoff leads Gordi over the low end of the poles a few times. Later he tries the higher side and Gordi can step over them without difficulty.

"Very good! Gordi has learned something. Don't forget to praise him!"

After a while we attach the chain from the other side and lead the horses from the right.

"That feels really strange!" says Shanti. "I feel as if I had never led a horse before!"

"That's why this exercise is so important for horses and handlers. It trains your body to transfer what you have learned from the left to the right. This activates both sides of the brain and improves your learning ability – and not just in the riding arena."

Riding bareback teaches balance

or me, riding without a saddle is e most natural thing in the orld. Without a saddle, you're ose to your horse, and you can el him more directly. When ou're riding bareback you can el each movement, each twitch f the skin, and all the big muscles orking underneath you. You can el the horse's warmth and even s breathing.

As a child on our farm in anada I rode bareback a lot. I as often asked to bring the orses in from the pasture, and hen I got to the herd I would mp on the back of one of the orses and ride in front of the hers – often with only a halter nd lead rope or perhaps just a ad rope around the horse's neck.

Mounting may be difficult for ou in the beginning. You may eed to mount with the help of a nce. When I was very young I arned to swing up using the ane and often the horse ran after e others the very moment I vung my leg to mount. I felt like ne of those daring Russian ossacks my grandfather had told e so much about. It was also eat fun to jump bareback. And ere's nothing better for teaching more stable seat. You really learn keep your balance and develop good sense for the rhythmic otions of your horse.

How comfortable it is to trot areback depends on your horse's ack, his gait and your seat. orses with a hard trot throw you o more. The faster you go, the ore difficult it is to sit to. The ow, comfortable jog of a Quarter orse is easy to sit, but the centuated, stronger trots of her breeds make you bounce ore.

To sit the trot bareback I like to ride American Indian style – it's the most comfortable way. The native Americans first saw horses when the Spanish came to America in the sixteenth century. When they met the first men on horseback they thought they were seeing a six-legged being. They perceived horse and rider as one from the very beginning – maybe this first impression somehow contributed to the fact that many Indian tribes became excellent horse people. Even though they used Spanish tack when they could get it and also made their own saddles and bridles, some tribes preferred riding without a saddle.

To sit the trot bareback, hold the mane and lean back a little, with your legs slightly forward. You can sit even a fast trot this way. Try it yourself!

Here's an exercise for bareback riding: move your seatbones from side to side with each step your horse takes with his hind legs. This way you can softly go with the movement of your horse's back at a slow trot. Another great

At a glance

Riding bareback

What is it? Riding without a saddle.

What is it for? To improve the rider's balance and coordination; to feel a more direct contact with the horse and to feel his movements better; to improve the rider's seat.

What does it do? With no saddle or stirrups to support the rider, she is challenged to keep her balance more than when in a saddle. She learns to follow the movement gracefully and to be in tune with the horse mentally. Bareback exercises with eyes closed are especially good for developing awareness of your body.

Caution! Bareback riding is a skill to be learned! Let someone lead your horse in an enclosed area at first, until you feel really confident. Since you don't have the support of the saddle, you may want to hold on to the mane until you can keep your balance without pulling on the reins or gripping with your calves.

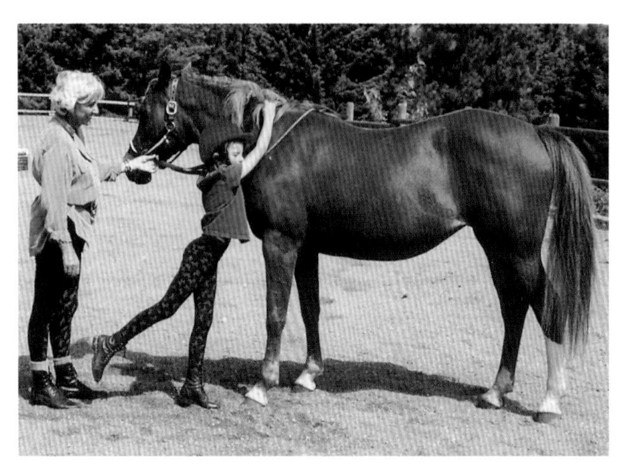

Mounting bareback: Shanti holds the mane with both hands and swings her leg right leg back.

The leg swings forward as she pulls herself upward. A well-trained horse won't move away. But just to be safe, have someone hold your horse.

Shanti is careful not to kick the horse's back. She is as agile as a cat!

Well done! Don't be discouraged if you can't do it on your first try. The horse might be too big for you. In this case let someone give you a leg-up or find a stable mounting block.

exercise is to raise your knees, bring your toes up so that the foo is flat, slide back a little behind th withers and post (rise) without a saddle.

But let's not start trotting right away. First I want to give the children a chance to really feel their horses and to do some exercises for balance. For this purpose we have built a new ground obstacle: the Zigzag. The curves in the Zigzag are not as tight as in the Labyrinth, but the horses do still need to bend.

Balance training

"Who wants to try the balance exercises first?"

Shanti is immediately thrilled. Agile as a cat, she swings up ontc the horse's back.

"Aren't these exercises just for beginners?" asks Geoff.

"Oh no! I know that you're all experienced riders. Shanti and Talia compete in lots of jumping classes."

"How do you like the exercises?" I ask Shanti.

"I like them a lot!" she replies. "Usually when I ride I need to pa attention to where my horse is going and focus on the riding lesson. I love just being led and feeling the horse."

I understand Shanti very well. Our attention is often on outside matters when we ride. We need t keep a safe distance from other horses, and keep an eye on our surroundings. These exercises wi help you to trust your horse. You can close your eyes and focus yo attention within. How is your breathing? How do you feel the movements of the horse? Is your seat stable or do you lose your balance quickly? How softly can you follow your horse's movements?

◄ 1 Shanti holds the mane as she closes her eyes and concentrates fully on the movement.

2 I am supporting Shanti to help her feel safe while she lies back. ►

▼ 3 She relaxes on Erin's neck at a walk.

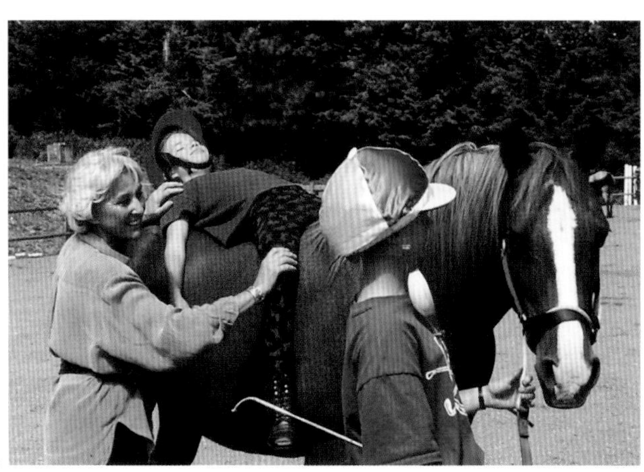

▲ 4 With eyes closed Shanti is led through the Zigzag.

◄ 5 Sitting backwards is fun and great for balance.

6 Playing possum! Is she really asleep? ►

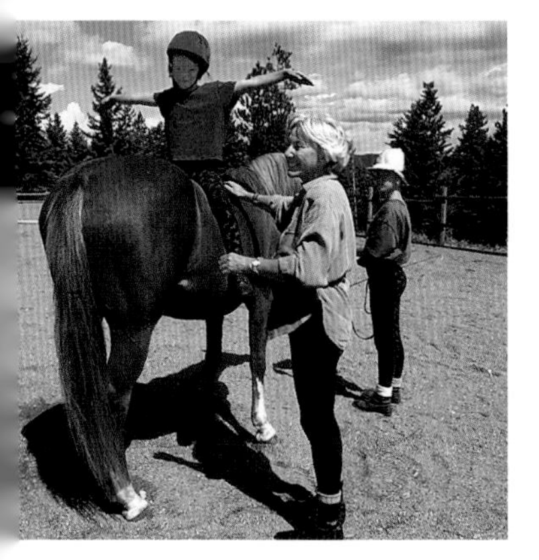

◄ 7 "Arms up and to the side. You are doing great!"

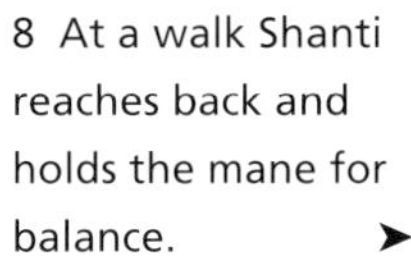

8 At a walk Shanti reaches back and holds the mane for balance. ►

9 "Sitting sideways is great fun. Can you imagine riding side-saddle?"

10 Sideways at a walk: the challenge is to always keep your balance and to follow the horse's movement.

11 Ready for the circus. What an athlete!

Linda's Tip

Mounting without a saddle

Not everyone can jump onto a horse's back like Shanti (see page 60) – and not every horse likes it. If the difference in height between you and your horse is not much you can try to mount like Mandy in this photo: she jumps up from the side, leans across the horse's back, supports herself with both hands, moves the right leg over the horse's back and sits up. You can make it easier for yourself by having a helper give you a leg-up. In England, mounting blocks are very common and no one feels embarrassed about using them. They understand it's often better for the horse. Don't make mounting unnecessarily hard for you or your horse.

Shanti is concentrating hard as I lead her through the Zigzag for the first time. I can tell how much she enjoys the contact with Erin. Now all the children want to get on a horse and try the exercises.

The horses are wearing halters with a lead line and a pair of rope reins attached, so that the rider can control the horse, if necessary. Added to this is a balance rein – a soft rope used in conjunction with your regular reins – around the horse's neck. Because none of the Aspengrove horses have been ridden with one before, we want them to learn to slow down and stop from pressure on the balance rein. The children are leading each other and are taking turns leading and riding. Of course the handler has to watch out for the rider and stop the horse immediately if the rider starts to slide off. It's important to choose a safe, quiet horse. These balance exercises would be much too dangerous with a nervous horse who couldn't be controlled from the ground. Only try these exercises with a calm horse in a safely fenced-in riding arena.

First do the exercises while the horse is standing, until you can c them well. Then you can do ther while the horse is moving.

The horses can also learn from these exercises. Not only do they

The children are taking turns leading each other at walk practicing the balance exercises.

go over the ground obstacles, but they also balance the rider's weight. You can use all the obstacles: the Labyrinth, the Star and the Zigzag. This keeps the work interesting for the horses.

Once everybody has done all the balance exercises we bridle the horses. Now the children ride without being led. Some of them are riding bareback for the first time. It's beautiful to see how secure and stable they are now.

We begin to work over poles. This improves the rhythm and the concentration of the horses. After a few tries at the walk some riders are already trotting over the poles.

"One hand on the mane! This makes it easier to keep your balance!"

Sitting the trot without a side-stitch

"Linda, I've got a side-stitch!" complains Allison as she brings her horse to a walk.

I know what it feels like: a stinging pain in the side after sitting the trot for a long time, with or without a saddle. I think that muscle tension and holding the breath cause this pain. To avoid it I suggest an exercise for Allison that can only be done bareback: trying to tense up in the trot on purpose.

"Tilt your pelvis backwards, let the legs come in front a little and tighten your buttocks as much as you possibly can."

"How awful!" Allison tries it immediately. "I'm bouncing up and down like a rubber ball!"

"And now try the opposite. Sit consciously relaxed and loose. Now you can tense and relax your buttock muscles intermittently."

Allison does the exercise, but it still looks as if she is holding her breath. I want to encourage her to breathe: "Count the footfalls of the horse's front feet out loud!"

At first, Allison can hardly say a number. But the more she relaxes, the louder her voice gets.

"Well, do you still have a pain in your side?"

Allison shakes her head as she rides by and keeps counting easily. If you can learn to sit relaxed and to breathe rhythmically with this exercise, sitting the trot will be much easie for you.

When riding bareback it is important to sit in balance and to make sure that you are not gripping with your calves. Insteac of using the thigh muscle many riders unconsciously grip with th calves. That only makes the horse go faster!

The legs can hang relaxed wher you're riding bareback, but it's important to practice closing you thighs for balancing around corners or in case your horse shie suddenly. To do that bring the knee up a little while your buttocks slide a little further back Tilt your foot until the heel is hel slightly lower than the toe.

If you need more stability, for instance when trotting over poles you can close your thighs. This way you'll have a stable seat without a saddle.

1 "You don't need to keep your heel this low. Feel how tight your calf muscles are in this position and how that stiffens your ankle."

2 "Bring the heel up a little until your foot is almost level. Also be aware of your hands. A straight line from the elbow to the wrist to the bit is best."

3 "To make you stable when riding bareback, the knee comes up a little, the thigh has a close contact, and your knee points straight forward. This position also helps when turning."

ːiding through the Zigzag promotes balance in horse and ider. Shanti rides Erin in a halter and practices light signals vith her calves and hands.

The children are riding in a bridle with a neck ring. This prepares the horses to be ridden without the bridle. The horses are learning to bend through the Zigzag.

rotting over poles teaches a stable, independent seat. Talia rides Drummer Boy on loose rein as he trots calmly over the poles. For a safer seat Talia could bring her nee up a little more to have a closer contact with the thigh.

Linda's Tip

Riding with a Lindel (TTEAM training tool)

You can ride a well-trained horse with just a halter through the Labyrinth. But to have a little more control, you can also try it with a Lindel or sidepull. It's a bitless bridle with a stiff rope nosepiece and a soft, adjustable, leather strap under the chin which doesn't apply leverage. The reins are attached to the side, instead of under the chin like on a bosal, making the signals clearer for the horse. Try it out, most horses really like it!

It gives you and your horse a break from riding with a bit. The horse can relax and lengthen his neck. It is particularly useful for a horse who is too sensitive in the mouth, or one who brings his nose too close to his chest. It's also an excellent tool for training young horses.

Riding through the Zigzag

Mandy uses a neck ring to guide her horse through the Zigzag. This TTEAM tool is an adjustable ring made of stiff rope that goes around the horse's neck. Once the horse knows the Zigzag all the children lay their reins on the horses' necks and guide them around the curves with the help of the neck ring. To go to the left, you touch the right side of the neck with the neck ring. The neck ring is usually used half-way between the chest and the head. If the horse doesn't respond to the signal, slide the neck ring up higher toward the head. It is amazing to see how quickly horses understand signals from the neck ring and to realize how comfortable they are with it. This use of the neck ring can be compared with neck reining in Western riding. The rein is held in one hand and taken over the neck to lead the horse to the opposite side. Of course, a horse is not only ridden with reins; shifting your weight and giving leg aids are also important. Often cowboys need both hands for their work, when they're roping a calf, for instance. Then, they can only give signals with their seat and legs.

Exercises for using the reins

Learning about 'soft hands'

There are different ways to ride with a snaffle bit. Some disciplines of riding demand a constant contact with the horse's mouth, others a relaxed rein, but it's always important to have a soft hand.

"How can I learn that?" asks Claire.

"By putting yourself in the horse's position!"

"You want us to put a bit in our mouths?" Talia asks.

"Not quite! But you can wear a bridle and hold the bit in your hands."

The children organise themselves into "horse" and "rider" pairs for a little experiment.

"Try moving the bit lightly back and forth, just the way the horse's head moves with it. Ask your partner – your 'rider'– to follow this movement softly with her hands."

Each "rider" sits opposite the "horse" and does various exercises with her hands.

"What's it like if I hold the reins with a closed fist?" I ask my "horse" Geoff.

"It's awful!" he complains immediately. "The hand is very hard and can't follow the movements at all any more. If I was a horse I couldn't go forward!"

When I hold the reins my hand is cupped as if I am holding a little bird in my hand. I don't want him to fly away but I don't want to squash him either. A closed fist is not just

"Human horses" who feel the effect of a bridle with their own bodies will later ride with increased awareness and a softer hand.

Ready to go! "Horse" Mandy is eagerly waiting for the signals.

"Horse" Claire would like to trot off with her head held high.

uncomfortable for the horse, but for the rider as well. The finger joints and the wrists are blocked by the tension, because all the joints in the body are connected. The tension in the hands continues on into the arms and shoulders all the way into the pelvis, and it inhibits breathing. I one joint is locked, it will influence the flexibility of all othe joints in the body, and locked joints make for a stiff rider.

Here is another exercise:

The "horses" wearing the bridl walk. The "rider" walks behind the "horse" and leads with the reins.

"Try different ways to stop

Angie says

All riders should imagine what it feels like to have a bit in their mouths before they hold reins in their hands. A horse's mouth is very sensitive – provided it has not been made numb by constant pulling on the rein. Don't allow this to happen! Pretend to be a horse and feel in your own body how much a hard hand can hurt a horse's mouth. Reins are not made for you to hold onto in order to keep your balance. Always remember that pulling on the mouth hurts your horse.

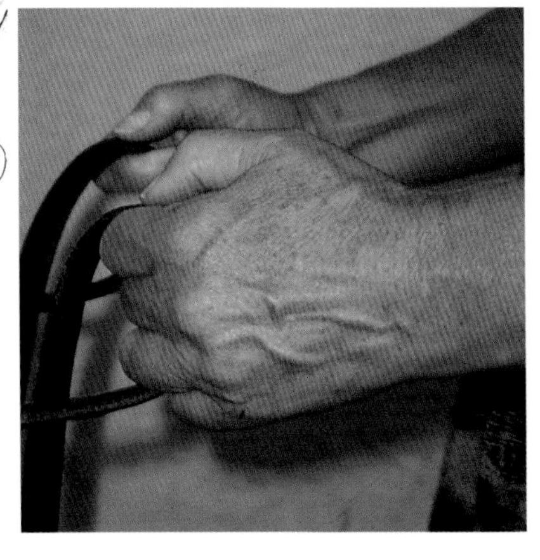

Correct hand position with a bridle: the wrists are straight, the thumbs are forming a small roof.

Not like this: the wrists are bent, the fists are clenched and the thumbs are flat.

our 'horses'."

The children are walking round the stable yard practicing ı a playful manner.

"I can't believe I can feel such ·ght signals!" says Talia after the xercises.

"It makes me think how I ɔmetimes pull on the rein!" Geoff ays.

"Once you've practiced this xercise you'll have much more ducated hands. I wish all riders vould try this exercise to know ow it feels to be the horse."

Correct hand position with a double rein. Hold the knuckles even and the hands slightly open for light hands.

Closed fists make hard hands.

Linda's Tip

How to educate your hands

Paint small lips on your thumb and the side of the first joint of your forefinger. Use them to keep your hands soft and check the way you hold the reins even while you are riding: the thumb forms a small roof on top, the hand is lightly opened and not clenched, the wrists are straight.

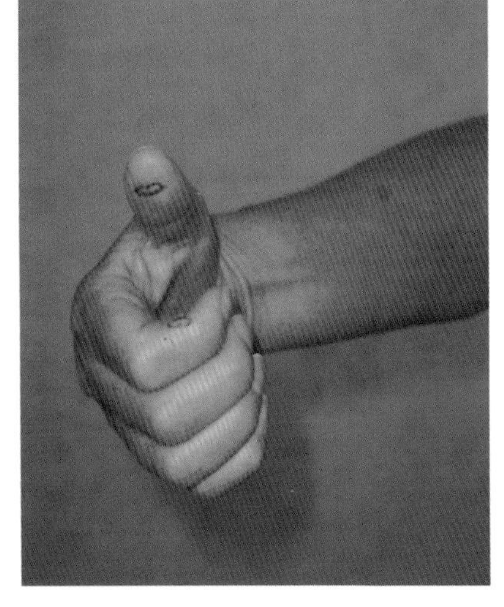

Do you see the small painted lips on the thumb and forefinger?

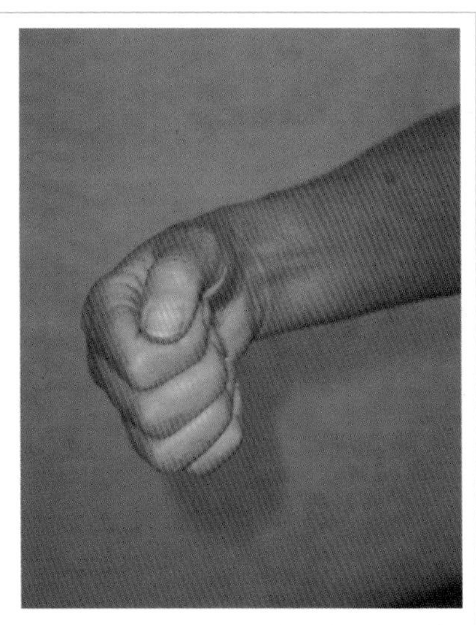

They are kissing: the thumb meets the forefinger where you painted the lips.

Bridling and unbridling

Here, I'm showing two different ways to bridle your horse. If your horse lowers his head willingly, you can bridle as I'm showing you in the photos on this page. If your horse raises his head, try the method shown on the opposite page.

In either case, it's important to put the rein around your horse's neck before you take off the halter. Notice how I'm opening the horse's mouth with my thumb and gently slipping the bit between his teeth with my index and middle finger. Take your time when bridling your horse and do it step-by-step.

1 (right) First I take off the halter and fasten it around the neck.

2 I put the reins around the neck behind the horse's ears.

3 My right hand is holding the headpiece and my left hand holds the bit in front of the mouth.

4 My thumb opens the mouth and I slide the bit between the horse's teeth.

5 I gently push the ear forward and lift the headpiece over it.

6 I close the throatlatch so that there is a space four fingers wide.

7 Check you can fit two fingers under the closed noseband.

utting on the bridle – for a horse who raises his head

My right hand holds the horse's head o make sure he won't throw his head ıp.

2 I lift the headpiece high enough to slide the ears under it.

I make sure not to bend the ears and ıently push them forward.

4 I check the bridle from the off side as well.

Angie says

Did you know that horses can feel homesick or miss their owner when they are sold. When you buy a new horse it may take him time to adjust to the new surroundings. He may be depressed, stubborn or afraid until he gets to know and trust you. Do you remember how you first felt going to a new school or moved to a new neighborhood? Use the TTouch to make him feel at home and to like you.

Removing the bridle

I steady the horse with my right hand on the reins as I slide the bridle down the horse's forehead.

Visiting the Haflinger stud

Bareback riding lesson

"We have an okay from Michael Davies!" Robyn greets us the next morning with this good news. Michael Davies is the owner of Fohlenhof, one of the most beautiful farms in the area. Fohlenhof is not only an excellent riding school but also a stud farm. Michael breeds and rides Haflingers, horses from Austria. I am delighted that the children have the opportunity to get acquainted with this breed.

"Who knows about Haflingers already?"

Only Mandy has seen Haflingers before, since they are not very well known yet.

"I am sure you will like them. They used to be the pack and carriage horses of the farmers in the Alpine mountains of Austria. They are very sure-footed and patient. Through cross-breeding with Arabians they've become a lighter riding horse."

"Can they jump?" Talia wants to know. She loves jumping, so the topic is always of interest to her.

"Of course! And Fohlenhof has a big cross-country course with all kinds of jumps."

Now everyone wants to go immediately and soon we're on our way. Fohlenhof is very picturesque and the horses are kept beautifully. We visit the broodmares in a huge pasture with their foals. Mr Bundschuh, the director, gives us a tour of the tack room. We admire the original Austrian festive harnesses for two- and four-horse carriages, polished to a perfect shine and artistically decorated.

"Can we ride?" Shanti wants to know, when we're in the stables with the school horses. Big dark Haflinger eyes are looking at us curiously from beneath long, thick, white forelocks.

"Yes!" Mr Bundschuh is very helpful and soon we're leading the horses outside.

Mandy is leading Axel, a seventeen-year-old breeding stallion. He can be ridden with all the mares and geldings without any problems. But suddenly he bends his front legs and wants to lie down on the green grass! Mr Bundschuh quickly helps Mandy, who is quite surprised.

"Axel knows a few tricks for shows," he explains. "One of them is to lie down. You probably gave him the signal without knowing it. Or maybe he misunderstood you..."

Mr Bundschuh laughs and pats the beautiful chestnut stallion on the neck. This shows us again that horses can be trained to respond to a variety of signals. Each riding discipline uses leg aids differently. An American saddlebred horse is usually taught to canter with a nudge from the rider's inside leg forward, whereas other horses are taught to respond to the outside leg being taken back.

"And which is right?" Claire wants to know.

"Both! Every riding style has value, or else it wouldn't exist. Many years ago my German dressage instructor jokingly said that you could train a horse to canter on the right lead by spitting on his right ear!"

The children are amazed, but Mr Bundschuh smiles and assures us that we don't need tricks like

The Haflinger stallion, Axel, knows a few tricks for shows. Lying down is one of them.

Festive harnesses and traditional Austrian bridles adorn the tack-room walls.

at to ride his horses.
The children mount bareback nd take a little time to get to now their horses. Riding single le and keeping a length apart is reat practice, but when we only de that way, the horses get too sed to simply following one nother.

"Let's try riding in pairs stead. Each rider has to take her orse out of single file and change mpo. She must slow down hile her partner catches up, or peed up around the corners hen on the outside. The horse arns to move independently, llowing signals from his rider, ot following other horses."

The children ride in pairs at the alk, trot and even canter a few ounds. The Haflingers are well-ained and cooperative. "Circle round the obstacle and keep an qual distance from one another. end your horse around your side leg and make sure his oulder doesn't drop to the side."

After a few rounds the riders reak the circle and ride rpentines around the jumps.

"Come down the bank at a walk nd let your horse step carefully ver the log. Stay about two horse ngths from each other, and take e log on a looser rein. emember what we've practiced: ise your knee, close your thigh nd the upper part of the inner lf against the horse. Lift your e until your foot is almost level. old onto the mane until you feel mpletely safe."

The children do well, keeping eir balance and going uphill and ownhill effortlessly. The horses so are having fun, and articipate attentively.

"Now for the bridge. Stay in alk and go straight onto it."

The first few horses step onto e bridge with no hesitation.

Bareback riding lesson with the Haflingers. It's fun and good practice to play at cavalry drill.

Mandy leads the group. "Go in a circle and be sure to keep your distances."

Talia and Mandy make a great pair.

"Downhill and over the log. Great spacing! That's nice, Mandy! You are giving your horse enough rein to stretch his neck and judge the obstacle."

1 **Over the bridge:** Mandy's horse steps over the Bridge without hesitation.

2 Claire's Haflinger is a little nervous, so I walk with him.

3 After a few steps he gets used to the sound of his hooves on the boards.

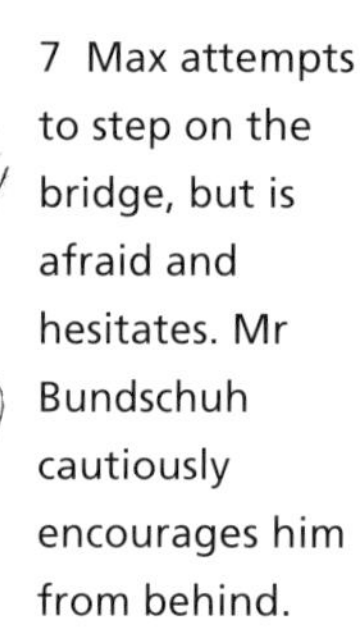

Angie says

I wish there were glasses you could wear to see the world with your horse's eyes. I'll bet you'd be very surprised! A horse's field of vision is very different from a human's. Horses can see almost all the way around themselves, but only a very small area directly in front of them is focused.

Horses also see some things later than we do or in a different perspective. So please be understanding if your horse shies at something that doesn't seem at all threatening from your point of view.

The Haflingers in these photos and their riders have very different views of the Bridge. The bushes that suddenly appear in the horse's view on the side make him feel insecure. From a horse's point of view every bush could be a hiding place for a predator who is stalking him. He inherited this instinct from his ancestors in the wild. When horses gain self-confidence they lose this fear.

I wish all riders would have enough compassion and understanding of nervous horses to get off and lead them a few steps under such circumstances.

7 Max attempts to step on the bridge, but is afraid and hesitates. Mr Bundschuh cautiously encourages him from behind.

8 I help Max to put his foot down on the bridge. This is also useful when you are loading a horse in a trailer.

"You're doing great, Geoff! Just keep
m coming slowly."

5 "Hold onto the mane if it makes you feel a little safer. That's a nice job for the first time over the bridge!"

6 "Shanti, dismount and lead your horse if he is afraid."

Max steps on the bridge hesitantly
ıd examines it with a low head.

10 Shanti holds the reins with both hands and walks at the horse's head.

11 They did it! Shanti is happy about her success.

hey don't mind the clatter of
ıeir hooves on the wooden
oards. The next few horses are
nsure, and refuse to go on.
"Dismount and help your horse
get over his fear," I suggest.
Lead him over the bridge the
rst time," I say to Shanti.
Shanti has dismounted and
ants to lead her gelding, but
lax won't set foot on the wooden
lanks. With patience, and help
om us, he finally goes on. Most
ders are taught to stay on the horse no matter how much the horse resists. Sometimes a horse's fear can be interpreted as disobedience, and a rider can start to fight with the horse. This is how accidents happen. The Haflingers wouldn't have been afraid of the bridge if we had taken them through the Confidence Course (see page 74) beforehand. Horses who shy, who are afraid of being loaded in a trailer, or of water, bridges or flapping plastic, don't need punishment, they need training. If my horse is afraid of an obstacle, it's because I haven't adequately prepared him for it.

"Linda, may we take the young Icelandics through the Confidence Course this afternoon?" asks Mandy.

"That's a great idea! We have all the materials we need for the Confidence Course at Robyn's. But let's practice with the horses here before we go back to the Icelandic horse farm."

Confidence Course

"Higher, higher!" The kids are cheering on Amadeus who's having great fun on the trampoline. On our lunch breaks the trampoline is like a magnet, drawing the kids to blow off steam. I'm looking at the dark clouds gathering in the sky. "Let's get started before it rains." Soon we're back at work.

To learn groundwork you break the work into the smallest possible steps. If it's your goal to ride a horse over a bridge, start with a wooden deck lying flat on the ground. If your horse doesn't want to walk across the full length of the platform, lead him over the short side. You can use various

The children are having fun on the trampoline.

leading positions. The Homing Pigeon often works well. Once your horse is walking quietly and confidently over the platform sideways, you can make the task little more difficult by going across the full length. When this goes well, we can add the rails. Finally, we can hang plastic sheet on the rails. A horse who can wal confidently over a deck with flapping plastic won't have a problem carrying a rider over a bridge. After exercises like this a horse loses his fear, even of being loaded into a trailer. Especially if you've walked him over, under and through plastic. Years ago, while teaching a clinic on trail competition, the usefulness of groundwork became very clear tc me. One of my students brought an Icelandic gelding, who was

1 We use two Zephyr leads for the Homing Pigeon with a young horse.

2 "Keep your wands at the same level, so that your horse ca focus on them."

5 Some oats on the platform help Hekla to lower her head, chew and breathe.

6 "What a good girl!" The brown mare follows Geoff and Claire and walks calmly over the platform.

specially difficult. At home he ad run away with her many mes and I was concerned he vould bolt in the clinic. For safety easons, I advised her not to ride ie horse during the week-long aining, but instead to work him om the ground over the bstacles. The gelding learned a ot, and relaxed a little. He hadn't een able to back up before and ouldn't trot; he paced most of the me. When we worked him over oles, he learned to trot and ained some self-confidence. But ow would he respond under addle? On the trip home the orse developed a cough and ouldn't be ridden for several eeks. His rider continued to do roundwork with him. When he ot well and she began to ride im again, she barely recognized him. He was calm and relaxed under saddle and trotted quite well. To her surprise, she could now back him up under saddle, and he had lost his tendency to run away. This experience taught me how useful groundwork can be for training a horse to be safe under saddle, so I developed the Confidence Course.

I use many different obstacles: tires, teeter-totters (see-saws), the Star, plastic and many more. When a horse can be easily led through the obstacles, put a saddle on him and lead him through again. When this becomes comfortable, then ride him through. Many trail competitions in America use a teeter-totter (see-saw) as an obstacle. Groundwork is great

Angie says

Do you ever wake up on the wrong side of the bed? Are you sometimes in a bad mood and can't even say why? Sometimes horses feel like that, too. They have good days and bad days. Some days your horse may not feel well, possibly from stiffness, soreness or pain. Instead of scolding him and punishing the "stubborn mule" who just "doesn't want to work today", be nice to your horse. Take a little time for some soothing TTouches, go for a walk with him or give him a rest. Remember: "Do unto your horse as you would have him do unto you!"

The young mare is insecure and jumps over the platform stead of stepping on it.

4 Claire lets the mare drift too far to the side and Geoff gets left behind.

When the two handlers aren't in 'sync' the horse receives nclear signals.

8 The next time Hekla has gained so much confidence that she walks over the platform lengthwise.

1 "Allison, be careful not to pull your horse around to the side. It'll be easier if you walk further ahead of the horse."

2 "Great job, Allison! Now you are exactly level with her head!" Eyglo is very attentive and faces straight forward.

preparation for trail tests. The judges are looking for good horsemanship as well as results. Imagine trying to participate in a trail test that included a teeter-totter, bridges and plastic with a horse who had never seen these items. It would be too much to ask. It's important to practice with these obstacles at home. Then you'll be ready to ride a new course, and both you and your horse will feel confident in the new environment. Even when you're just out riding, there are many things that will scare a horse who hasn't been well trained. It's so important to have safe horse, one who won't shy, who has self-confidence and enjoys working with you.

The children help Robyn bring in a few young horses who've ha no experience with groundwork.

I think groundwork is an essential part of training a young horse to be ridden. He learns to

At a glance

The Confidence Course

What is it? A series of ground exercises involving obstacles to help your horse overcome his fears and trust you in all situations.

What is it for? For basic training of green horses to train them to become safe riding horses; for skittish and nervous horses; to prepare horses for trail riding and trailering.

What are the effects? The horse learns step-by-step to master threatening situations. He gains self-confidence, learns to listen to you and overcome his flight instinct. He will become safe, courageous and dependable.

Caution! Always be prepared for a sudden move or jump to the side. Be ready to get out of your horse's way. Keep enough distance and stay alert and agile when you are working with these ground obstacles.

Linda's Tip

Groundwork with tires

Some horses are afraid at first to step directly into the tires. This is how you can make it easier for them: spread the tires out further so your horse can step in between the tires and then lead him through. Be careful with a horse who is shod. He can get his foot caught in the rims of small tires if he pulls back. This is a practical exercise to teach your horse to place his feet in a bucket in case you need to do it.

If a horse is insecure we can add two rails. "Keep the mare the middle of the platform."

2 Hekla examines the bridge and the food on it. "Geoff, step up little more, until you are level with her head."

espond to our signals and to ccept aids. A young horse who nows the meaning of "Walk", Trot" and "Whoa" from the round will be able to understand ou when you are in the saddle. ften a young horse doesn't nderstand what the rider wants. The horse doesn't know what the signals mean and won't move. Unfortunately, the rider often becomes impatient and gives signals that are too strong – like an undeserved smack with the whip. The horse is afraid and suddenly jumps forward and bucks. All this can be avoided by doing groundwork, because you will have found a common language you both understand. Your horse will know the meaning of the voice command "Walk" and a light tap with the wand. Groundwork gives you an

The young mare is suspicious of the tires. She paws at them d doesn't dare to go forward.

2 "See, it's not so bad! Take your time and look at it. Good girl!"

"It's easier with two people. She already has one foot in a e. Hold your lead line a little looser, Geoff!"

4 The mare understands and steps in the tire. Claire and Geoff show her the way with their wands.

1 "Come on, Hekla, you don't need to be afraid of the teeter-totter." Hekla doesn't agree and stops.

2 We change the teeter-totter to the platform, bring the rai out further and put plastic sheets on on them.

5 "It's just the wind rustling the plastic. Look around, girl, it's OK."

6 I do some circles on her neck to relax her.

8 I am stopping her on a straight line and am also asking her in the leading position Dingo to bring her hindlegs up on the platform.

9 Hekla responds to my signals and walks cautiously across the platform in the Dingo.

opportunity to win a young horse's trust and to establish a relationship with him.

It's good to work in pairs when starting with a young horse. Geoff and Claire are working with Hekla, a young mare who hasn't done any groundwork yet. At first she's afraid and doesn't want to step into the tires, but the children are patient. After a little while, she's learned to follow signals from the Zephyr lead and the wand and trusts Claire and Geoff. Now they lead her to the bridge.

"Can you take the flapping plastic down from the rails?" ask Geoff. "Our horse is a bit afraid of it."

"I'll remove the plastic sheets t

I come to help Geoff and take Hekla myself. "Look at the ‹astic, it won't hurt you!"

4 "Very good! Your front feet are already up on the platform. Come on, I know you are not quite sure of this."

A little Ear TTouch relaxes Hekla and ›lps her trust me.

At a glance

Ground obstacles with plastic

What are they? Working with sheet plastic: flat on the ground, as a raised alleyway, or as an obstacle to walk under.

What is it for? To teach horses to overcome their fear of noisy, moving things; for horses who are claustrophobic and afraid of movements above them; to prepare horses for loading in the trailer and trailering; for show horses who shy at spectators and flapping tents or flags.

What does it do? The horse loses his fear of foreign objects and unfamiliar noises. The horse gains more self-confidence, shies less and will be a safer trail horse.

Caution! Prepare your horse for each obstacle and keep a safe distance to be sure you won't get jumped on. I recommend using clear, sturdy plastic. Please recycle it when it can't be used any more.

ıake it easier for your horse to ›t used to the bridge. But ›ventually I want her to learn to ›alk over the bridge with the ‹astic on the rails."

›ften people want to make life ısier for their horses by simply moving anything that might ›are them. Some people never ›e a wand because their horse is ›raid of it. But by avoiding ›sturbing things, the horse never ›arns to overcome his fear. We ›uld skip the flapping plastic in ır groundwork but what will ›u do when you're out riding ıd a plastic bag lies in your way › a flag waves in the wind and ›akes a noise? Wouldn't it be ›eat to have a horse who isn't ›raid? Not only will your horse ›come safer by working with plastic, but he'll gain more self-confidence. Every time your horse overcomes a fear he'll become more trustworthy in all situations.

If your horse doesn't load into the trailer very well, you can help him by working him with plastic. Often horses are afraid to go under the roof of a trailer. You can practice walking under plastic with the help of two friends holding a rolled-up plastic strip. Lead the horse underneath and slowly lower the plastic to make the task more challenging (see photos on the next page).

1 Eyglo stops and is afraid to go under the plastic.

2 She rushes through and Allison automatically tries to slow down with her elbow.

3 Allison quickly corrects herself and is rewarded by success.

Allison wants to practice walking underneath plastic with Eyglo, a light chestnut mare with a blaze. Claire and Talia are holding the plastic for her. Allison and Eyglo succeed the second time they try and Allison is very proud of the pretty horse.

"You really are a fast learner," she says patting her neck. "Now you know that you don't have to be afraid." The chestnut mare snorts softly and Allison has a big smile on her face.

The teeter-totter (see-saw)

Mandy teaches her horse to walk over the teeter-totter.

"You have done really well," praises Robyn. "I am sure the horses would be happy if all of you could come and work with them more often."

"I'd love to!" Talia is excited. "I really like the Icelandics. Maybe I can come back again soon."

1 Mandy allows Dumba to explore the teeter-totter with a low head.

2 Dumba advances slowly as she searches for scattered oats.

3 "Come on, just a bit more. We're almost to the other side."

ʌore fun with the Haflingers

ʌe wake up to cloudy skies the ext morning. It's cold and an icy ʌind blows around the house. he weather report doesn't give s much hope. "More rain and loudy skies" are the prediction.

"Do you think we can ride at all ı this weather?" asks Shanti.

"We wanted to jump the Iaflingers today and I was really ɔoking forward to it," says Talia.

I look at our photographer. What do you think, Hilmar?"

"Of course we'll go. The grass as a really nice color in the rain nd I am sure you'll be fine!"

Hilmar keeps inspiring us with is enthusiasm and when we rrive at Fohlenhof the weather as cleared up.

I am glad we are able to go jumping, too, because I love teaching it. I can really understand the children's excitement, since I had a passion for jumping myself as a young girl. I can still remember how I built a "wall" from bales of straw and jumped my Thoroughbred gelding Pride, over four feet riding bareback! In my experience, horses love to jump when they're trained in a way that they understand. I'm sure Pride had just as much fun as I did jumping over my "wall". Over time we won many ribbons together.

In my riding school and summer camps, I taught not just bareback riding but also jumping bareback. Most of my students learned it very quickly. Once you have a good, stable seat, it isn't difficult. Most children who ride love to jump. Even going over low jumps teaches them to balance and follow the movements of their horses.

Allison and Talia are jumping bareback for the first time. We warm up the horses and are trotting single file through the jumps on the beautiful cross-country course. The children are riding various figures in a walk

Angie says

Did you know that horses can only breathe through their nostrils and not through their mouths like you? Now imagine how a horse must feel if you cut off the airflow through his nostrils with a very tight drop noseband. Some horses experience a shortness of breath and panic! This is especially bad if the noseband is not only too tight but also sits too low on the horse's nose. When you do use a noseband, as is customary in many riding schools with school horses, please follow this rule: make sure you can fit two fingers between the horse's chin and the noseband.

llison jumps with a loose rein. "Great mp for the first time over! You could ring your leg up a little and turn it so at your knee points straight forward hich will give you more contact with ɔur thigh."

andy's thigh and the upper third of er inner calf are on the horse and give er the needed stability and security ver this jump, even without a saddle.

1 Talia's first bareback jump. She takes the jump in the "clothespin" seat, stiffening her leg and rounding her back.

and a trot. Then we ride towards the first jump. It's a natural fence which has varying heights in different sections. The children can choose how high they want to jump. It's an exciting morning! Talia has never jumped bareback before and slips off her horse. She lands in the soft grass without hurting herself. "I want to try it again!" she insists while she's still scrambling to her feet.

"Great! I'll show you what you can do to improve your seat. It's the same position we practiced yesterday, walking our horse over the log: bring your knees up, take your leg a little forward and don't stretch out your lower leg. Take hold of the mane for balance." At the end of the lesson Talia's seat has become much more stable as her horse flies over the jumps.

Claire even jumps holding both arms out to the side – and everyone applauds! Mandy does well, too. She has a lot of riding experience, but only with Icelandics. I am very proud of my niece who adjusts to the Haflingers so quickly and jumps in such beautiful style.

We've been having so much fun, we haven't even noticed that it's started to rain again. After a while we can't continue outdoors.

"You wanted to practice mounting and dismounting anyway," Mr Bundschuh says. "You can take Axel in the covered arena. He's already saddled up."

Axel is well trained and stands perfectly still for mounting. Most riders are accustomed to mounting facing the croup,

2 Ooops! Talia lands in the soft grass while her horse waits patiently.

3 "Your knee was stiff and your leg slid back, making it hard to stay on over the jump."

4 "Pull your knee up to give you more contact with your thigh and upper calf."

5 Wow! Halfi takes a huge leap and Talia clings like a burr! A great accomplishment for her first bareback jumping lesson.

Linda's Tip

Holding the mane

Holding the mane while jumping or riding bareback is not just for beginners or insecure riders. Sometimes it's an advantage even for skilled riders: your seat is more secure, you don't bump your horse's back or mouth, especially over poles or jumps. Hold the mane as close to the roots as possible and hold it so you have a strand of hair between your index finger and thumb. Keeping your wrists straight and off the neck prevents your back from becoming round.

The balance exercises pay off. Claire's got a great seat and feels so secure, she drops the reins, stretches her arms out and closes her eyes.

·hanti shows she can do it, too. Up and over they go!

1 **Mounting with a saddle**: holding the reins and mane in her left hand, Mandy reaches over the other side and holds onto the saddle flap.

2 She mounts with grace. Mandy can balance herself well in this position.

3 Mandy sits gently down in the saddle Axel stands still and waits for Mandy's signal to go forward.

putting a foot in the stirrup and then swinging around in a half-circle to get up into the saddle.

There's an easier way to mount by standing parallel to the horse and facing forward. This way of mounting has many advantages:

- You are not pulling on the back of the saddle, which puts your horse off balance, over time twists the saddle tree, and puts unnecessary strain on his back.
- You won't accidentally poke your horse's side with the tip of your boot.
- In most cases this way of mounting is more comfortable and actually easier for the rider.
- Your horse finds it easier to stand still.

It hurts your horse's back when you fall into the saddle. Your horse will drop and hollow his back – the very thing we want to avoid. With horses who have sensitive backs it is even more important for the rider not to thump into the saddle when mounting. Many horses won't stand still for mounting because they were never trained to do so and lose their balance when riders are not coordinated or careful about climbing aboard.

Linda's Tip

Balance exercise

This is a good exercise to help find a balanced seat and the correct angle of your pelvis. Reach with your right hand to the tip of your left foot and then with your left hand to the tip of the right foot. But be careful: don't let the opposite calf slip backwards. Slide your seat backward in the saddle like a ducktail, otherwise you'll lose your balance and fall forward. If this exercise is hard to do, your stirrups may be too long. Shorten them until it's easy to reach your toes.

With a little practice and agility you can adjust your stirrups with one hand even at a trot or canter.

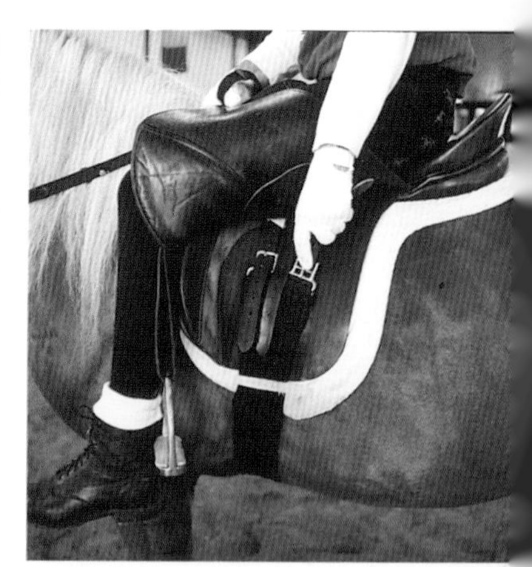

Tightening the girth is best done when the horse is standing or, with a little practice, on a safe horse in a walk. You should take your foot out of the stirrup

Riding the school horses

"It's stopped raining!" Hilmar says. "Let's drive across the valley to Aspengrove and use the good light in the riding arena."

We take Axel back to the stables. Mandy removes the saddle and leads him into his spacious box, where his feed is waiting for him. We say good-bye to the Haflingers and thank Mr Bundschuh.

Amadeus wants to ride

"Can't I ride, too?" asks Amadeus on the way to Aspengrove. He is the son of my co-author Andrea Pabel and the grandson of our photographer. He's only five years old and hasn't participated in our riding lessons.

"Why do only the bigger

Dismounting: Take the reins and ıane in the left hand, put the right and on the saddle, take both feet out f the stirrups and prepare to vault off.

Mandy springs lightly out of the ıddle.

1. Amadeus tries out some balance exercises."How far forward can you reach? All the way to the ears?"

2."What a nice place for a nap!"

3 "When I stretch my arms I can reach up this far!"

Angie says

"He always acts up when I put the saddle on him," people say when a horse holds his breath or tries to bite when you girth him. How would you feel if someone tightened your belt suddenly! Would you like that? Your horse doesn't either! Please tighten the girth slowly and with consideration. On a tense horse it is very helpful to do some Belly Lifts or Python Lifts in the girth area before you do up the girth.

4 Backwards? No problem for Amadeus with Mandy's support.

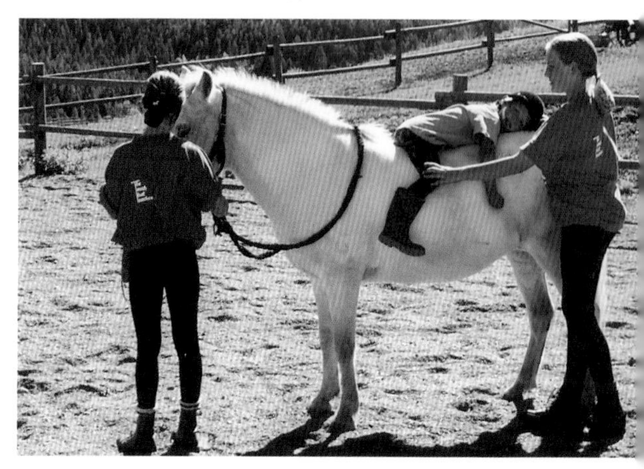

5 "You can lie down on Silver's croup this way, too." The gra mare likes children and stands still patiently.

6 "Can we walk a little?" Allison makes sure that Silver doesn't walk too fast.

7 Amadeus likes sitting sideways. It is a good exercise for balance and courage.

8 "Can you lie on your stomach and stretch your legs all the way to the croup?"

children get to ride?" he asks me.

Perhaps you have heard this question before. Almost all little sisters and brothers, and neighbors, sooner or later want to ride too. Maybe you find the little ones annoying at times and you think they're just in the way.

"What would you like to do with the horses?" I ask Amadeus

"Gallop!" he says with sparkling eyes. "That's what I do at home with Mom's horse!"

Do you remember how happy

Amadeus wants to show what he can
o.

10 Trick riding must run in the family!

11 Of course, always wear a safety helmet.

ou were when you finally got to
ıde for the first time? And how
ard it was when all you could do
ʼas watch? Take some time out
ɔr the little ones! Get them a
elmet that fits and sturdy shoes
nd put them on a quiet horse
ou can trust.

That's what we did with
madeus. The gray mare Silver is
ıst the right height for him and
madeus' joy rewards us all. He
as a natural seat and no fear.

In England, North America and
ustralia it's very common to put
oung children on horseback. In
ears past I've taught six-year-
lds to ride over very low jump
ɔurses on safe horses. Many
orses love small children and can
e great nannies. Some children
ven learn to ride before they can
alk, and sit in the saddle with a
atural ease many adults can only
ish for.

Mandy, Robyn's daughter, is a
reat example. She takes after her
other, who loved to explore the
orld from horseback as a small
ddler. Mandy "rode" for the
rst time when she was just six
eeks old! Robyn and Phil took
er riding in a backpack at least
nce a day. Even though, at home, she often didn't sleep well, she dozed off as soon as she was on the horse. When she was a year old, her parents put her in front of them in the saddle. Then, at two years she rode on her own with one of her parents "ponying" her. It was no surprise to hear that Mandy trained her first horse when she was barely eleven years old.

My sister Susan started to ride when she was three and showed my jumpers when she was seven years old in junior competitions. Of course, all young children need to be closely supervised and should only ride in a safe, enclosed area.

After he has done a few balance exercises, Amadeus rides Silver through the Zigzag by himself. You can tell how proud he is to be able to guide the gray mare alone.

Breathing exercises

While we've been in the arena with Amadeus the others have already brought the horses in, groomed and saddled them. In the arena we first spend a few minutes doing TTouch on our horse's faces to deepen our contact with them and to do something nice for them. Remember that a horse is a feeling being so don't treat him like a bicycle. He is happy when you greet him and spend a little time with him before you ride.

The children mount and we do a few balance and breathing

Angie says

Often horses enjoy small children because young riders are usually very kind to them and are not as heavy as adult riders. Many horses even take extra care of children. Some horses act like nannies, being very gentle and especially careful. As soon as a young rider starts to slide in the saddle, they stop so she won't fall off. Of course, not all horses are this patient and calm. And where you can make a difference is with the TTeam work and the TTouches. Of course, all inexperienced children need to be supervised by adults.

1 "Your seat is so secure that you certainly won't need the reins for support." Amadeus picks up the reins which are attached to the halter so he can practice his aids without pulling on the mouth.

2 Amadeus guides Silver through the Zigzag with Allison far enough away to give him a feeling of independence but close enough for safety.

3 Amadeus confidently guides Silver through the Zigzag without help.

4 A proud five-year-old rider on the back of an experienced twenty-six-year-old mare.

5 Amadeus has great fun going over the poles like the bigger children.

exercises. It's so important to breathe well while you ride and not to hold your breath. If you do, you not only tense up yourself, but your horse also feels your tension.

I learned about breathing exercises for the first time from my grandfather George. He spent many years living in the far north of Canada. It's very cold there and the winters are long with lots of

The children are leading the horses through a wood going down to the riding arena.

ed in their own areas, the horses can be groomed and
ıddled at a safe distance from each other.

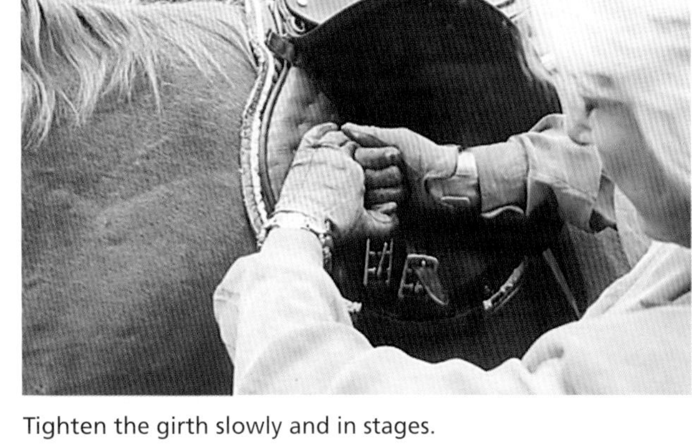

Tighten the girth slowly and in stages.

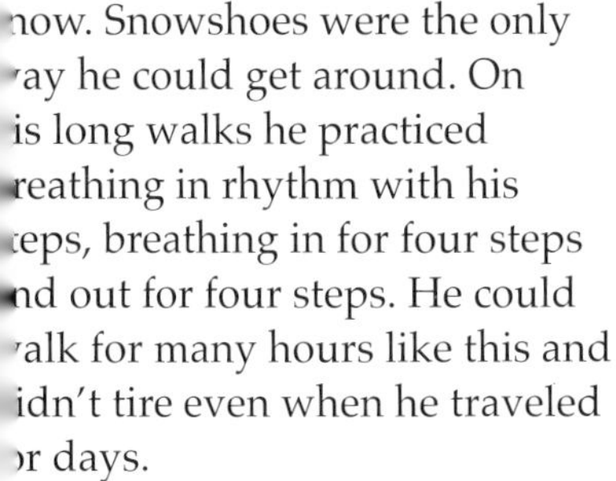

now. Snowshoes were the only
vay he could get around. On
is long walks he practiced
reathing in rhythm with his
teps, breathing in for four steps
nd out for four steps. He could
valk for many hours like this and
idn't tire even when he traveled
or days.

This breathing exercise is great
or riding. You can practice on a
orse by counting every footfall
ut loud: "One, two, three, four."
When you have developed a
eeling for this rhythm you count
ilently and breathe out for four
ootfalls and breathe in for four
ootfalls.

Now you can do the same
xercise at the trot. Breathe in for
our footfalls and out for four
ootfalls.

It's fun to see how many steps
ou can go before breathing out. I
njoy experimenting with this.
or example, I'll breathe in for six
ootfalls and out for six footfalls,
r go eight in and eight out. You
an also breathe in for six footfalls
nd breathe out for eight footfalls.
n order to do this you'll have to
reathe deeply from your lower
elly.

I've seen many riders improve
heir balance and seat with these
reathing exercises.

You can learn to relax your
nuscles and release tension in

The horses enjoy some gentle TTouches on their faces before we mount.

"Keep your spacing and hold your arms out to the side." This is great practice for confidence and control.

What fun! Riding three abreast at the trot.

1 "This foot position gives you a secure seat for posting (rising to the trot). Think of the stirrup as the ground. When your heels are too low the knee moves up and down and you can't hold your leg still."

2 "It's better not to take your leg this far back. Keep the stirrup level with the girth for the greatest stability."

your back and shoulders. It's also great fun. In the beginning you may lose count occasionally, but soon you'll learn to focus on your breathing and develop a better feeling for the rhythm of your horse and your own body.

"Linda, I don't know what to do!" Talia is frustrated and trots over to me. "I just can't manage to hold my legs still when I am posting (rising) at the trot! My calf keeps sliding back. Why is that?"

"You're forcing your heel down too much and it's stiffening your leg."

I place Talia's leg in a more stable position.

Swinging legs make your seat unstable and can make your horse nervous. Imagine what it would feel like to be a horse and constantly have a rider's flapping legs hit your sides!

At home in California Talia jumps almost every day and has practiced riding with heels forced down. It's the accepted style for equitation. But when you post or rise at the trot your leg will be steadier if the heel is only slightly below the toe. Imagine that the stirrup is the ground you're standing on when you are in the saddle. The heel of your boot may be slightly lower than the tip. Often, beginning riders are told to keep their heels down, because they have a tendency to pull them up and so everyone tries to get the heel as low as possible. But when you are posting with a very low heel your knee isn't stable and moves around. This makes the entire leg unstable.

When your heel is just an inch or so lower than the toe your leg stays stable on the horse's body.

There are two different ways to

Linda's Tip

Posting (rising to the trot) with the motion of the horse

This is a good exercise to practice posting with the motion:

- Sit on the edge of a chair and keep your thighs parallel to each other.
- Imagine a plumb line from the middle of your kneecap to the inside of your foot.
- Now slide your seat back in the chair and move your head towards your knees while keeping your back straight.
- Lift your seat a few inches off the chair, pushing your seatbones backwards. Your knees open slightly.
- Now sit down again and practice getting up and sitting down a few times in this position.
- If you are in balance you will be able to stop at anytime, without falling backwards.

ɔst or rise: behind the motion ıd with the motion. Which you ıoose depends on the style of ding and the breed of horse.

- Trotting behind the motion ith contact on the rein will give ɔur horse more impulsion from e hindquarters. You can push m forward with your pelvis into e rein. The horse will be ɔllected and on the bit.
- To post with the motion eans to follow the horse's ovement. You don't constantly ush your horse forward because ɔu expect him to keep his tempo ı his own. You can have some ɔntact with the rein or ride with loose rein. Your pelvis is angled that your seat bones are tilted ehind you. The rising and sitting otion is caused by the opening ıd closing of the angle of your elvis to your thigh. The knee is able. The inner thigh and the pper part of the inner calf are in ɔntact with the saddle. You ɔn't need to rise out of the ıddle very far at all when you e posting like this. It's important keep your back straight and ɔt to arch it. On hunters and mpers you post with your body ightly forward and on ddlebreds or dressage horses ɔu rise with your body in an upright position.

I show Talia how she can steady her leg by imagining a pin holding the middle of her calf against the saddle and softening her ankle by not forcing it down so low. After a few rounds her seat has become much better. Of course, it's difficult to change a habit. Talia worked hard to learn to ride with an extremely low heel – and now she is supposed to do the opposite! But she finds that posting is easier with a softened ankle.

The balanced seat

There are many ways to ride horses and many good reasons for the different styles. That was one of my principles when I was training riding instructors. My students came from many different countries and had learned a variety of styles of riding. I didn't want to give them the feeling that they were riding "incorrectly", just because they hadn't learned the American balanced seat that I was teaching. This balanced seat was developed by the US cavalry from a combination of the Italian *Caprilli* style and the French *Cadre Noir* seat. The American cavalry needed a seat that was comfortable for both the horse and the rider. They had to ride for hundreds of miles without changing horses. It was crucial that the horses didn't go lame. A rider who sits in balance helps his horse to stay sound.

Many years ago a pilot who had never ridden came to me for riding lessons. I gave him the usual simple instructions on how to sit and how to hold the reins. He looked at me and asked "Why?"

For a moment I was speechless. When I stopped to think about it I didn't really know why. No one ever said why we ride with the elbows in and the heels down. I either had to quickly make up an answer or admit that I didn't know myself. I decided to ask my husband this question. As an officer in the US cavalry with excellent riding training he would certainly know the answer. He delivered a long lecture to me and at the end I knew one thing, he didn't really know why, either! What did it really mean to have a good seat? What did balance on horseback really mean? Many riding instructors limited their

ɔtting in the balanced seat: I'm sitting slightly forward, allowing me to follow the ovement smoothly.

I'm sitting more upright here.

instructions to these five commands: "Sit up straight! Keep your heels down! Keep your elbows close to your sides! Hands one hand's width above the withers! Look straight ahead!"

If the student didn't understand these instructions the riding instructor just yelled a little louder. No wonder it took the average person so many years to ride well using this method.

I had to find my answers myself. So I began to compare different styles of riding, always looking to find a common principle, a basis of balance. How could I give a rider detailed instructions for better and more successful riding?

In the years that followed I constantly dealt with this question and developed an instructional manual called *Thirty-three Points of the Balanced Seat* for my riding teachers. The real answers to my questions about balance I only discovered later in my training as a Feldenkrais practitioner. Today, I have developed my method for teaching the balanced seat even further and I call it the "Joy Of Riding".

With this method a rider can adjust to a variety of different riding styles, by using a different saddle, changing the position of the leg, the length of the stirrups or the position of the foot in the stirrup. In my training center the students didn't just learn one way of riding, but learned how to ride and compete in dressage, Western classes, endurance rides and jumping – all on the basis of the balanced seat.

The seat of the rider changes with the gait of the horse and the degree of collection of the horse. When I ride a horse in a collected canter I sit with a little longer stirrup, a straight upper body and a deeper seat in the saddle. I have my foot in the middle or to the outside of the stirrup. If I want to influence my horse more with my pelvis and my calves I can take my leg back. There are slight variations depending on the saddle.

If I want to gallop or jump I must change my seat: I shorten my stirrups, slide my seat back a little, keep my back straight and tilt slightly forward. I feel like my seat is floating above the saddle. My weight is distributed on the inside of my thighs, the upper half of the inner calf and the widest place on the ball of the foot. This seat is very good for young horses or horses with tight backs or undeveloped muscles.

I think it is important to be able to adjust your riding style and seat to the horse, the saddle and the situation. If you only know how to ride dressage you will have difficulties riding a Western horse. If you only know how to jump, you might have trouble riding a gaited horse. On my travels around the world I've ridden horses of all breeds and have always adjusted to the way they were ridden. I can just as easily ride a hunter in England as

You can reach forward like this by pushing your pelvis back in the saddle to keep your balance. Horses like TTouches on the neck a lot. If you've prepared them with the TTouch from the ground they will lower their heads under saddle and relax. This exercise is good preparation for jumping.

Remember to really praise your horse while you work as well as afterwards. Here the horses are enjoying some well earned gentle strokes.

ne balanced seat in the canter. Look at the rein and note the :raight line from the elbow to the bit and the horse's mouth.

Here I am holding the reins between my thumb and index finger. This is unusual but allows for a soft hand while cantering and jumping.

the canter and while jumping I put ore weight on the inside of the irrup. The contact with the inside of y thigh and the upper third of the side of my calf gives me the necessary ability in the saddle.

gaited horse like a Paso Fino om South America or a dressage orse, such as a Hanoverian or ldenburg from Germany. The alanced seat allows me to be exible and doesn't limit my ding possibilities.

Recently, while on safari in otswana in Africa I rode a ddlebred for eight hours every ay. I took time to experiment with different seats, various stirrup lengths and foot positions. Sometimes I tried to keep my feet directly under my center of gravity. Then I changed my seat and took my feet a little more forward. (This is how American and Australian cowboys often ride.) Their saddles are made especially for this seat and distribute the weight of the rider over a larger area. I found this to be very comfortable at a walk and my horse was relaxed. In the trot or canter, still experimenting, I changed my seat again. I shortened my stirrups and sat a little more forward. I found this seat to be very safe when the situation asked for being on guard, because Cape buffaloes would sometimes charge out of the bushes and scare the horses. I was prepared for a sudden leap forwards, a sideways shy or bolting. The horses were not overly spooky, they were just protecting themselves. It's the only way to escape a charging Cape buffalo or hippopotamus!

Even if you're not on safari, this adjustable balanced seat is very useful. It improves your breathing because your diaphragm is free and relaxed. Your back doesn't

Linda's Tip

Picking up your stirrups

Who hasn't desperately "fished" for a lost stirrup? Everyone knows you shouldn't look down to "catch" it; you will not only lose your stirrup but also your balance. So how do you pick it up again quickly?
This is the easiest way: knock against the stirrup with your foot. It will swing to the inside a little. As it swings back outward catch it with your toe. Don't give up if you don't succeed at your first try. It does take a little practice!

have to work so hard because you use fewer muscles to keep your balance. And, it helps the horses to be comfortable, too.

A riding class in the beautiful arena at Aspengrove. The school horses are well trained and in excellent condition.

Trotting over poles on the ground

"Can we trot over those poles back there?" asks Mandy towards the end of our riding lesson.

"You read my mind! I was just going to suggest that as our next exercise."

Trotting over poles is a great exercise for balance and a good preparation for jumping for both horse and rider. The horse gets used to the colorful poles and learns to keeps his rhythm as he trots straight over the middle of them. Once your horse is used to the spacing, try it on a loose rein. Horses who are trained on a loose rein don't need to be driven over jumps and don't run out or refuse – they learn to jump safely and willingly.

Balance exercises in the saddle. "Put one hand on the mane and don't arch your back while you are standing in the stirrups."

The horses are trained to stand quietly on a loose rein, while their riders continue the balance exercises.

"Reach for the tip of your left boot with your right hand. Push your pelvis back in the saddle so you don't fall forward

Trotting poles not only serve as preparation for jumping. All horses, no matter what discipline they are used for, can benefit from them. This exercise encourages rhythm and improves the gaits of the horse. The rider learns to jump without depending on the reins for balance.

The children and horses are having fun trotting over the poles. Mandy leads the group and holds her arms out to the side. Talia tries it, too. To do this the girls need a very stable seat – and they

'alia trots Drummer Boy on a loose rein. This exercise mproves the rhythm of the horse and the seat of the rider.

"Hold one hand out to the side and stand up a bit in the stirrups to free your horses' backs."

Can you rise slightly out of the saddle and hold your arms vithout losing your balance?"

Happy horses and riders. Posting (rising) at the trot over the poles with their arms out to the side. This is what I call balance!

hanti demonstrates the balanced seat ery nicely: the plumb line from the hip ɔ the foot is clearly visible. Notice the traight line from the elbow to the orse's mouth. She is looking straight head and follows the movement of her orse with ease.

›bviously have it. They're aughing as they trot over the ›oles and are even holding hands o test how well their horses stay ogether!

Riding with a neck ring

"Today we're riding with the neck ring again!" I announce in the morning.

"Can you ride horses with just a neck ring and no bridle?" Geoff asks.

"Yes, I'll show you how you get them used to being ridden with the neck ring only. Most horses learn it very quickly. Of course, we only ride with the neck ring in a safely fenced arena. Since we've already ridden with the neck ring a few days ago through the Zigzag, the next steps will be easy."

We lead the horses into the arena and I help Talia switch Drummer Boy from a bridle to a neck ring. You need your wand for riding with the neck ring. Your horse already knows the signals you can give with the wand from the groundwork exercises. To be safe, we must get the horse used to the neck ring step by step.

- First Talia rides with a bridle and the neck ring.
- When she can stop and turn the horse with the neck ring with the reins tied on the neck, I take a thin twenty-one foot rope and tie it around the horse's neck with a bowline. This is a special knot that won't tighten if a horse pulls back and it is also easy to release.
- I take off the bridle and make a halter from my rope. I take a

I show Talia how to use the neck ring to stop and turn while Drummer Boy stands quietly.

"Begin riding with the reins tied on the neck. To turn left, you lay the neck ring against the right side of the neck. Your right hand gives a little pressure, while your left hand lifts up slightly."

At a glance

Riding with a neck ring

What is it? Riding without a bridle, using a neck ring made from stiff rope joined to make an adjustable ring round the horse's neck.

Tools The wand clarifies signals given with the neck ring.

What is it for? To develop trust, to improve a horse's balance, gaits, attitude and disposition; great for horses who are high headed, overbent or tight in the back; wonderful for the rider's balance, confidence and communication with the horse.

What does it do? The horse moves more freely, relaxes his neck and lengthens his stride. The rider improves her seat and learns not to use the reins for balancing. This is fun for both horse and rider.

Caution! Practice riding with a neck ring in an enclosed arena. You need someone on the ground to help you prepare your horse to be ridden with the neck ring only. Make sure you go through the steps outlined in this book so you are safe and can always control your horse.

Preparation: I am using a long light rope (about twenty-
•ne feet) to make a halter to lead Talia at first.

2 The step-by-step preparation gives security. Drummer Boy responds willingly to Talia's signals.

The light rope is now only around the neck and I am
/alking with Talia to be on the safe side.

4 "You can stop with a signal from the neck ring, by closing your thigh and using a voice command. Do not press with the lower leg to stop."

5 Now Talia is able to guide Drummer Boy with the neck ring only, even at a trot.

›op of the rope in the direction of
ıe chest and then pull it from
ehind through the loop around
ıe neck and slip it over the nose.

Then I make a second loop and lay it over the loop already around the horse's nose.

• I hold the rope about ten feet away from Talia's horse while she's giving the signal with the neck ring.

• To stop we use three signals:

1. Slide the ring up higher on the horse's neck and give gentle pull-and-release signals for him to stop.

2. At the same time, close your upper thighs and make yourself lighter in the saddle.

3. Give a voice command: "Whooa."

• When the horse stops easily from these signals, I remove the loops from his nose and continue to hold the rope loosely from about ten feet away.

1 **Signals:** To reinforce your signal to turn you can hold the wand out to the side and gently tap the horse's face.

2 "Great, Mandy!" Xanidu knows the signals with the wand from the groundwork and understands what Mandy wants her to do. She is being ridden with the neck ring for the first time today!

• When she's riding well at a walk and a trot, I take off the rope and Talia is ready to ride without my assistance.

"This feels great!" Talia is thrilled. "I have to try this out with Oliver when I get home! I'm sure he's going to love it!"

She praises Drummer Boy lavishly. "You've learned this really fast!"

6 Mandy guides her horse at the trot with only the neck ring. It's obvious that both horse and rider are enjoying this new experience.

The neck ring helps horses to stretch and relax. A good example was a horse named Justyn Thyme. The thirteen-year-old gelding was a member of the German Olympic Team that won a gold medal in three-day eventing at the Seoul Games. His rider, Claus Ehrhorn, asked me to work with him because his shoulders and back weren't as flexible as they used to be.

When I watched Claus ride Justyn Thyme, even on a loose rein the gelding wasn't able to stretch his neck long and low. I did some TTouch work with him and then rode him in a neck ring. Without the bridle, Justyn Thyme was suddenly able to relax and lengthen his neck! His movement became more fluid and he could move more freely from his shoulders. Claus rode him in a neck ring on a regular basis for a few weeks and a month later they were first after the dressage phase at an international three-day event in England. Justyn Thyme not only had his old form back, he was even better than ever before!

Jumping with a neck ring

"Can we jump the horses with a neck ring?" Mandy asks.

"Of course!" I have vivid memories of jumping my mare Angel without a bridle when I was a teenager. In the sixties, when I had my school for riding instructors we gave jumping demonstrations without bridles. We rode Hungarian warmbloods – a mare, a gelding and two stallions – and our displays created a lot of excitement and admiration.

Years later I demonstrated jumping without a saddle and bridle at the huge annual horse fair, Equitana, in Germany. The audience was very surprised to see someone riding without a bridle. Many said: "This is impossible! We've never seen this before!" No one could believe tha

3 Mandy bends her horse around her inner leg and rides a small circle to the right.

4 "You raise the neck ring to stop. Then you give pulsating signals with it and...

5 ...tap your horse's shoulder. Praise her when she stops and release the pressure on the neck ring."

such a relationship with a horse was possible.

Today, riding with a neck ring is quite common and normal in Germany, Austria and Switzerland. It makes me happy to think how many horses and riders have gained a deeper relationship through this. You can't ride with a neck ring unless you've mastered the art of communicating with your horse without force. It is a wonderful feeling to guide your horse without a bridle. It is an

1 I love riding horses for the first time in the neck ring. Soon I won't need the bridle any more.

2 Trotting in the balanced seat: Xanidu trots for the first time and follows my signals willingly.

3 Cantering with a neck ring is great fun! My mare enjoys her free head without the bridle.

4 Now we all ride with neck rings. Nobody wants to stop and we ride until it gets dark.

Mandy trots Xanidu over the poles. Her position is lovely: her knee is straight ahead and her leg close to the horse.

"And now one hand out to the side. Very good, Mandy!" Xanidu keeps her rhythm and is trotting over the middle of the poles.

With the neck ring, Xanidu willingly jumps over the cross-poles. I am following her movement and hold the neck ring loosely.

expression of harmony and friendship.

"Today we'll be working with trotting poles again to start with!" I tell the children.

Once they're doing this well I set up a small jump with cross-poles. I put trotting poles in front of the jump. The poles should be four feet to four feet six inches apart, depending on the size of the horse, but the most common distance is four feet six inches. For a small pony, about three feet six inches may be correct. Leave one pole out before the jump so it is nine feet from the jump to the first

Mandy and Cody jump for the first time with the neck ring.

Yeah! Look, no hands, no bridles!"

Pair jumping without bridles. Drummer Boy is a little concerned, but Talia and Shanti keep perfect timing.

ɔole for normal-sized horses of ıbout sixteen hands.

The trotting poles are one of the ɔest methods for teaching a horse o jump quietly and safely.

The children practice over the rotting poles in single file and in ɔairs with their arms out.

"Now we can do another ɔreathing exercise," I suggest. 'When you are riding toward the ump count the footfalls out loud: ɔne, two, three, four! This way 'ou make sure you're not holding your breath over the jump."

"Is it so bad to hold your breath a little?" Shanti asks.

"Try it," I suggest. "Jump and hold your breath on purpose, then jump again and breathe out over the jump. You can even sing!"

Shanti tries it. "When I hold my breath I'm less flexible and can't go with the horse's motion very well," she says, surprised.

She jumps again. This time she counts out loud. "This is much easier and more fun!" calls Shanti and trots towards the jump again with sparkling eyes. There's no hesitation, no insecurity. She knows she can count on Erin. They are flying over the jump. Shanti takes Erin back to a walk and praises him: "You've done really well!"

Erin snorts and stretches his neck for a moment of relaxation. Then he puts his ears up attentively. "And what are we going to do now?" he seems to be asking.

Mandy rides Cody

'he next day we return to \spengrove to ride once more. 'his time Mandy rides the Quarter Horse gelding, Cody.

"His neck is so tense, what hould I do?" Mandy brings the 'hestnut over to me.

I take a closer look at him. He is ·we-necked and doesn't seem to ɔe able to flex in his poll. Mandy s riding him in a snaffle.

"Let's try a balance rein on ıim," I suggest.

"How did you ever think of ısing a balance rein?" Allison ısks as she watches us adjust the ıew piece of equipment.

"In one if my clinics I had a very difficult warmblood. He would twist his neck to avoid contact with the rein and was very difficult to control. He was a valuable horse, but since he was considered unrideable he'd been sold from one show barn to the next. I tried him in a TTEAM training bit and it helped a bit, but he still twisted his neck and was too strong at the trot and canter. Then I suddenly had an idea. I took the lower rein of the TTEAM training bit over his head and put it around his lower neck. I used it like a second rein. By pulling

Cody is ewe-necked and tends to drop his back.

1 Mandy reaches forward to do some TTouches on the neck. Cody gives and rounds his neck.

2 Cody's neck improves at the walk.

3 In the trot he falls back into his old habits: he raises his head and tightens his neck and back.

4 When Mandy touches his neck he remembers what he has learned, engages his hindquarters and rounds his neck.

Linda's Tip

How to hold the balance rein

In the beginning it will feel awkward to hold both the balance rein and the bridle rein. The photos here show you two ways of holding the reins:

a) When your horse pulls, have a bit more contact on the balance rein than on the bridle rein.

b) If you need the balance rein to steady a spooky horse every once in a while, it may be easier to hold it the second way. Wearing gloves will be more comfortable.

(a) Hold the balance rein between the ring finger and the little finger, and your bridle rein on the outside of the little finger when using more contact on the balance rein than on the bit. Useful if your horse is nervous, pulls on the bit or has an unsteady trot.

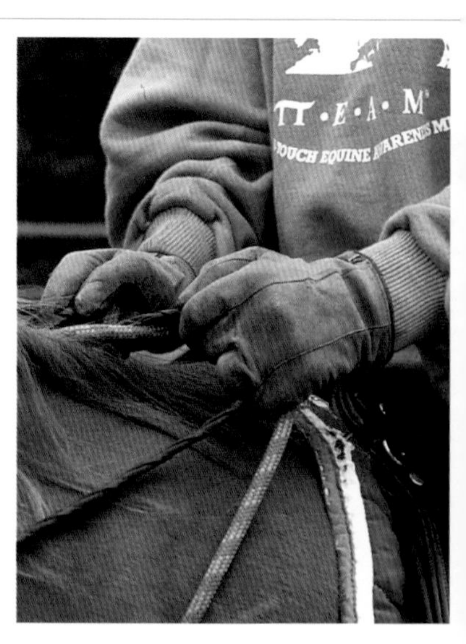

(b) Hold the bridle rein between the ring finger and the little finger if you expect to use mostly the bridle rein and only occasionally balance your horse around corners.

gainst the neck and combining it vith a signal on the top rein the horse responded quite differently: was able to slow him down vithout him twisting his neck. His back became more elastic and he was wonderful to ride. I called ny invention the balance rein because it helps horses to come nto balance."

"Should I use the bridle more or he balance rein more?' asks Mandy.

"Fifty percent balance rein and ifty percent bridle in the beginning. You can also reach orward and massage his crest with one hand from the saddle. This will help him learn to lower his head and lengthen his neck. When Cody has difficulty bending in the corners you can correct him with the balance rein. Use the balance rein on the inside of the neck so that his shoulder doesn't fall to the inside of the bend."

Mandy does a great job and Cody improves a lot in the walk. But in the trot he falls back into his old habits and tenses up.

"Let's try him in the TTEAM training bit," I suggest.

At a glance

Riding with a balance rein

What is it?

A rope placed around a horse's neck made either from a seven foot long, half-inch wide rope or a twenty-one foot long, quarter-inch wide rope made wider with a chain stitch as shown in Linda's Tip on this page.

What is it for?

For horses with a tendency to go too fast and who don't respond well to the bit to slow them down; horses with hard mouths; those who are too much on their forehand or go above the bit; and to help ewe-necked horses.

What does it do?

The balance rein is used in combination with the normal bridle reins. It causes a high-headed horse to lower his head, lengthen his neck and raise his back. You can collect your horse more easily and he can use his hindquarters more actively. You'll notice your horse's balance improving.

Caution!

It takes practice to use the balance rein together with your regular reins. Don't give up! The balance rein must fit properly. If it's too long, you'll hold your hands too high or bring them too far back, which will can throw you off balance. If your horse is sensitive, use the wider balance rein, made by chain stitching the rope (see Linda's Tip).

How to make a wider balance rein

Some horses respond even better to signals from the balance rein when it is wider on their neck. You can easily make a wider balance rein by taking a rope about twenty-one feet long, quarter-inch wide and chain stitching it as shown in the photos. Notice, do not chain stitch the parts of the rope where you hold it with your hands.

At a glance

Riding with the TTEAM training bit – the roller bit

What is it? A type of pelham bit with a port and a copper roller which most horses enjoy – that's why it's called a roller bit. It has long, curved shanks, a curb chain, and is ridden with two sets of reins.

What is it for? It's wonderful to ride your horse in the TTEAM training bit to improve his balance and gait. It's really useful for re-schooling ewe-necked horses or horses who are hard mouthed, who don't like a bit, who are stiff or stubborn, shy, buck, or are highly strung.

What does it do? It softens the mouth, jaw and poll so the horse can be more flexible in the neck, more elastic in the back and free in his movements.

Caution! The training bit is not to be used like a snaffle! Neither rein should be held tightly, especially not the lower one. Normally you let the lower rein hang loose. Use a light hand or your horse could become overbent, and the beneficial effect of the roller bit will be lost.

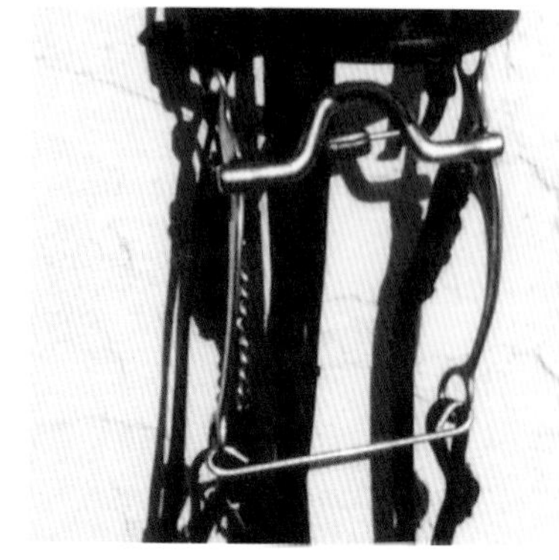

This is what the TTeam training bit looks like: a type of pelham with a port and copper roller.

How not to hold the reins of the roller bit! The wrists are bent, the thumbs flat and the hand is closed to a fist.

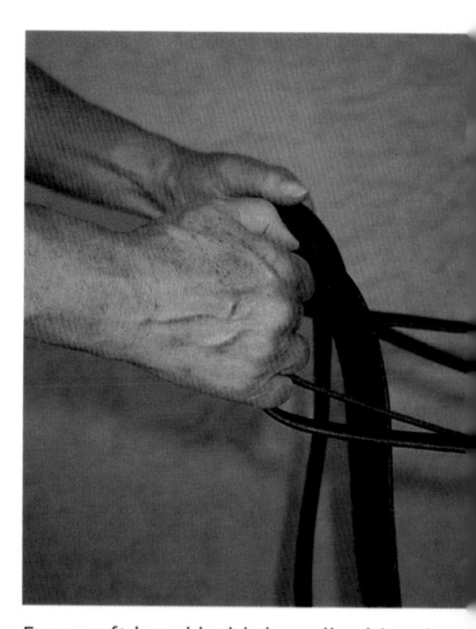

For a soft hand hold the roller-bit reins like this: straight wrists, fingers softly closed and the thumbs like a little roof on top.

"Oh, yes. I've never used one before," says Mandy.

We put the TTEAM training bit on Cody. It works very differently from a snaffle bit. It has loose curved shanks, a wide curb chain and a small copper roller in the middle of the port. It's ridden with double reins.

Most horses like this bit a lot. They soften in the mouth and it foams easily. Of course, it has to be fitted correctly. The bit has to lie in the horse's mouth so that there's a visible wrinkle in the corners of the mouth. Make sure that the bit doesn't touch the horse's molar or wolf teeth. The curb chain should be adjusted so that when the bottom rein is tightened the shanks of the bit are at a forty-five degree angle to the line of the mouth. The curb chain should lay flat.

By using the TTEAM training bit most horses become more elastic in their backs, are able to flex better in their polls and engage their hindquarters.

"Linda, look how well Cody is doing!" Mandy calls after riding him a little.

Mandy has very soft, sensitive hands and just the right touch for a difficult horse. The bit belongs in the hands of a rider who doesn't have a strong hand, but can give light signals with soft fingers.

"Do you think I should ride him

ody's carriage has improved in one session. With the neck ring, the gelding relaxes his back and engages is hindquarters. Horse and rider will feel much better like this in any gait. A great success!

vith a neck ring now?" asks Mandy, now that Cody is doing o well with the TTEAM training it. He engages his hindquarters, engthening his neck and moves n balance.

We take off the bridle and use he neck ring again. Now Cody noves very well with the neck ing at the trot. What a change! Often it doesn't take very long for horse to learn something new. Many people assume that horses re stupid and can only learn by epetition. I have heard that often myself but it's been my xperience that horses are often able to learn very fast – much faster than most people think is possible. Horses get bored by being lunged for long periods of time, with the same lesson repeated over and over. Some horses resist this boring routine – and often people don't understand why. Imagine how unpleasant it must be to keep having to do a lesson you understand and can do well, over and over again.

Cody has learned this lesson in three quarters of an hour. A beautiful success for horse and rider!

Angie says

If your horse refuses to go forward and pins his ears back he may well be in pain. Has he been out for a very long ride or to a strenuous competition the day before? Horses do get sore! Many horses who buck, run away, or bite, act this way because they are in pain. Before you punish him or call him "difficult" or "mean," check the horse for sore areas. You wouldn't like to carry a heavy backpack if you had back pain, would you? If your horse is stiff or sore, help him with the TTouch.

Riding the Icelandics cavalry style

We spend our last day with the Icelandics. When we arrive, Robyn is working with a young gelding. "He's a little nervous around his hindquarters so that's why I want to put a body wrap on him to make him feel more secure," she explains.

"This is a great TTEAM tool and it will be interesting for you," I say.

The children watch as I help Robyn with the body wrap. At first the pretty chestnut gelding is a little insecure, but he soon relaxes.

"The body wrap helps horses to feel safe and to get a better sense of their bodies. It also calms a horse for a farrier or vet visit."

"Can you ride a horse in a body wrap?" Geoff asks.

"Yes, you can. The body wrap has proved very helpful for horses who are insecure on rides and shy a lot."

"Are we are going to ride again, Linda?" asks Talia.

I know how much the children are looking forward to one more riding lesson. We catch the horses, groom and saddle them up.

"What signals are the Icelandics used to?" asks Claire, who is already in the saddle. "They're not ridden like the school horses, are they?"

"No, they're trained a little differently. I'll show you how you ask them to walk.

- Give a little pressure with the upper part of your calf and then release. Your horse steps forward on the release, not while you press.
- Your hand opens a little to allow the horse to move forward.
- You make yourself a little lighter in the saddle and free the horse's back.

"But I learned this very differently," says Talia. "We sit deep in the saddle and push the

1 The Icelandic gelding Penni is nervous about movement behind him. This is why Robyn uses the body wrap on him.

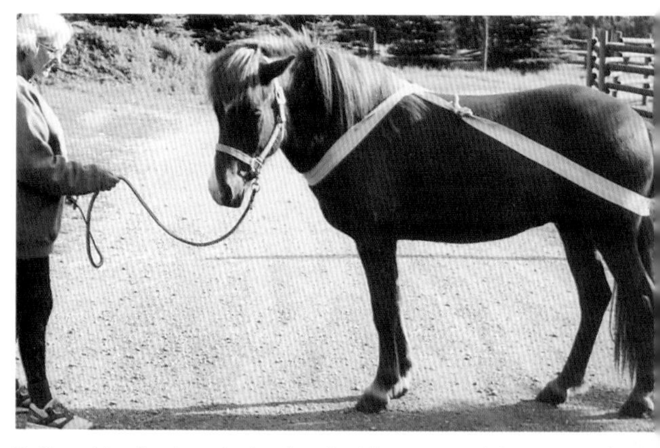

2 Penni looks skeptical: what is this strange thing around my hindquarters?

3 Because Penni was nervous we first put the body wrap over his tail.

4 Now the young gelding feels more confident and we can put the wrap under his tail above the gaskin.

Linda's Tip

My horse won't go forward

I often see a rider who pushes with her seat and bangs her horse's sides with her heels or presses up with her heels to get him to move forwards. The horse mostly responds by throwing his head up, dropping his back and not budging! If you do have to get him forward quickly, it is much better to take the reins in one hand and give your horse a loose rein while you give him light, quick taps behind with the wand. This way you won't pull on his mouth when you are reaching backwards with your wand. Tap him on the hindquarters, or behind your calf, to signal him to step forward. If your horse is already familiar with this signal from groundwork and you reinforce it with a verbal command he will understand what you want him to do. The best solution is to teach your horse from the ground to go forward from the Dingo leading position – stroking the back and tapping the croup. Then when you're in the saddle, a tap on the croup or loin from your whip will make your horse move forward willingly.

orse with our calves and seat ɔrward into the bit."

"This is another way to ride. It's ke another language. There are ıany different languages."

I explain that "thank you" in nglish and "danke" in German ave the same meaning. It's the ame with riding. Different styles f riding use different signals to ell a horse to walk. "The signals ve just given you are signals that re especially useful not only for celandics but for young horses vith undeveloped back muscles r horses with sore backs."

We are doing one more riding lesson with Robyn's Icelandics. Single file over the poles and on serpentines, each rider takes turns leading the group.

Claire tries the signals and gets along fine with her gelding. "And how do I stop?" is her next question.

"You close the thigh. At the same time you give half-halts. The half-halts are given only with your finger joints and a soft movement of the wrist."

"This works really well!" Claire is very pleased when her horse stops willingly.

We ride over to the Labyrinth. "You can practice turning your horse here." These are the signals I tell them to give:

- Before the turn shorten both reins a little. The outer rein has to give slightly, while you use the inner rein to give the signal to turn.
- Bend your horse around the inner calf.
- The outer calf is held a little further back behind the girth and keeps your horse's hindquarters from turning out.
- Turn your pelvis in the direction the horse is going.

Claire rides through the

Linda's Tip

Riding with a body wrap

After your horse has become used to the body wrap on the ground, you can use it when you ride as well. Make sure the wrap is not under the saddle. The body wrap has proved to be very useful with: skittish horses who are afraid of noises or shy a lot; horses who don't engage their hindquarters very effectively; and horses who hollow their backs.

Riding four abreast takes practice! We didn't quite fit over the cavaletti together.

These exercises are fun and the children are improving their seats and their aids while playing.

Around the corner Shanti has to slow her horse down while I have to let my horse move faster in order to stay abreast.

"In pairs, next to each other! Keep a safe distance between you. Good, Shanti, keep moving up a little until you are even with Claire."

Labyrinth without stepping over the poles.

"Now we'll ride single file and do an exercise I call "weaving-in-and out". Keep two lengths behind the horse in front if you and keep about six feet from the arena fence so another horse can pass between you and the fence. The last rider starts to trot and weaves in and out in serpentines between the other riders until she is at the front of the line. Now she needs to look back and take her horse back to a walk two horse lengths in front of the horse behind her."

The children try this exercise and find that it takes a lot of riding skill. We need to be able to judge distance and ride with precision. It's even more difficult when everyone is trotting! With practice we can do this exercise riding with half of the horses going around the arena in one direction and the other half in the opposite direction weaving in and out.

The riders learn to use their aids effortlessly and the horses learn to move independently.

"This must be a great exercise for herd-bound horses!" says Shanti. "There's a horse in my riding school who doesn't like to be away from the other horses."

"If you do these exercises with him a few times he'll learn not to be so herd-bound any more. You can also teach him to be more independent from other horses when out on rides. A great exercise is to have one rider go on ahead while the other rider stops and turns back in the other direction for about one hundred feet – then turns around and trots past you for about fifty feet and waits. You take turns going away from each other and coming back together until your horses get used to being alone at times. You

At a glance

Fun cavalry exercises

What are they? Various exercises that riders can do in pairs, threes, fours or in single file, riding different figures in the arena.

What is it for? To develop the accuracy of your aids. These exercises are fun for horse and rider!

What does it do? The horses learn to follow your aids and not cling to the other horses. These are things that you can learn or improve: to give aids correctly, to maintain distance and speed accurately, to ride independently, precisely and with respect for others.

Caution! Especially when trotting or cantering it's important to be aware of the other riders around you to prevent bumping into another horse. Keep an eye out and make sure to keep a safe distance at all times. I recommend riding in pairs only if your horses don't kick!

fast *tölt* with the Icelandics. This gait is so smooth that Geoff can hold a cup of ater without spilling even one drop!

can ride circles in different directions or separate at a crossroads. With time you will be able to stretch these exercises out and ride farther away from the other horses. This is how you can help a horse become less herd-bound."

To finish, we ride a few rounds at a *tölt*. This is a gait special to Icelandics. Tomorrow Mandy, Robyn and Phil are going to a big horse show in Montana in America to participate in competitions for gaited horses. The *tölt* is amazingly comfortable to sit and Geoff can hold a cup of water in his hand keeping it so still that he doesn't spill one drop while his horse zips around the arena!

Animal Ambassadors

It's time to say good-bye: Claire and Shanti have to leave.

"I want to give you a little present," I say and bring out my beaded pouch of little animals made from stones. "Maybe you know that many native American tribes had totem animals? A totem animal was a protective spirit for the person who dreamed of it. Some people met their totem in a vision. If someone had a vision of a buffalo, the spirit of the buffalo would watch out for that person, be his guide, and give him protection and strength. Now times have changed. Everywhere, animal species are being threatened with extinction and pushed out of their normal habitat by humans. Many animals on earth are in great need. They need your help! It's time to protect our animals, to be their totems and ambassadors. Everyone can choose one

Carved animals like this one are my gifts to the children as good-bye tokens.

"I have a seal!" Amadeus is happy.

animal from the pouch. You will be the guardian of this animal."

The children are passing the pouch around and reaching in with their eyes closed.

"I have a dolphin!" Shanti calls out and holds up her small animal.

"And I've got an owl!" says Claire.

The children show each other their animals and are delighted with their choice. "I'm going to take good care of my dolphin," says Shanti as she hugs me good-bye.

"You will certainly be wonderful animal ambassadors," I say. "You can do so much for them! Just keep caring."

"And for Pepper! He'll be very glad I came to this clinic with you. I bet he'll love the ear TTouch. I can't wait to try out everything I've learned here with him!"

You, too, can become an animal ambassador like Shanti. In the pages that follow you will find more information and a certificate to fill out.

By the time we've all said good-bye it's late afternoon. "I'd love to go out on a trail ride now!" says Mandy.

Geoff, Allison and Talia are thrilled by the idea. Soon they have their horses ready and ride off. They've asked Hilmar to take their picture while they're riding into the golden evening light and waving to all the readers of this book: "Good-bye!" They all wave and call as they disappear around the corner of the pasture.

"Thanks for a great time!" Allison on Eyglo, Talia on Sleipnir, Mandy on Djarfur and Geoff on Starjna wave good-bye as they ride off for a last ride together.

How to become an Animal Ambassador

Many North American native tribes believe they have animals who protect them. They are called "totem" animals. These animals are their allies and give them strength and power.

Today many animals are endangered and we need to reverse that situation.

Now, humans must become "totems" for animals to protect them, help them and care for them.

If you would like to join us and become an Animal Ambassador, choose one or two animals you feel a special connection with. Learn as much as possible about this animal and its needs, how it lives and what it requires to be healthy and content. What can you do to help and protect it?

You can cut out the certificate on page 121 of this book, fill it out and hang it in your room. It will always remind you of your special animal friends and the vow you've made.

The TTEAM philosophy

- To honor the role of animals as our teachers.
- To bring awareness to the importance of animals in our lives.
- To encourage harmony, cooperation and trust between humans and animals as well as amongst humans.
- To recognize the individual learning process of every human and animal.
- To respect each animal as an individual.
- To teach interspecies communication through the TTouch.
- To work with animals using understanding in place of dominance.

Why TTEAM is good for me

Ten reasons that will convince your parents

1. With TTEAM, being kind leads to success. The focus is on clear communication with the horse. Yelling and punishment become unnecessary.

2. I am becoming more self-confident through riding and am learning to assert myself with gentle means from TTEAM training.

3. TTEAM gives me a better sense of my body and improves my balance, because both hemispheres of the brain are activated by the leading exercises when I use the wand and lead chain together. Thinking and feeling are enhanced, coordination improved and the overall ability to learn increased.

4. With TTEAM, I experience over and over, how important patience and concentration are in reaching my goals.

5. I learn step-by-step to overcome insecurity and fear and master difficult situations. I learn to recognize aggression as a sign of fear. I teach horses to overcome fear rather than punish them when they bite or kick. I learn through the horse to recognize my own fear and aggression and learn how to override these emotions by thinking instead of reacting instantly.

6. A horse is like a mirror. He shows me through his reactions and his behavior how he wants to be treated. I'm learning to respect his particular personality. This is the only way real partnership and friendship can grow.

7. I'm learning to become aware of myself and others, to recognize my limits and to assert myself in safe, logical ways. At the same time, I experience the limits of others and respect them.

8. Since each horse is different I am learning to adjust to various personalities and peculiarities. I become more sensitive and emphathetic.

9. No matter how annoyed I get, I learn patience and self-control with the horses. I'm learning to handle frustration because with TTEAM I have so many choices to deal with a problem. I learn to be flexible and don't get discouraged.

10. With TTEAM I'm having fun and experiencing success. I'm with people who treat animals, people and nature with respect and support each other.

Children need horses

An afterword by Hans Schindler

As a family therapist, horse lover and father of five children, I have read this book with great enthusiasm. It is written in understandable language, imparts many very sensitive methods and encourages children without taking away from the respect and caution that is necessary when dealing with horses.

A relationship with horses and riding is an important experience for many children in their process of personal growth.

With horses, children gain self-confidence. They learn to communicate. Often just the feeling of being on horseback is enough to promote a child's inner-growth process. The TTEAM methods described in this book enable children to make themselves understood with gentle means. Mastering difficult situations helps them to overcome insecurities and fears. They see that these big animals sometimes react very fearfully, but that they can calm a horse. The strengths children learn here can be very helpful in other aspects of their lives, in school and with their friends. At the same time they experience limits, their own, as well as the horse's.

Linda Tellington-Jones' TTEAM method promotes empathy and respect for horses and other living beings. Respect and self-respect are like two sides of the same coin: whomever wants to be respected has to respect others. Children can learn how real partnership and friendships are made. They find that each horse has a different personality and that communication only happens if they are considerate of a horse's peculiarities. The horses provide them with direct feedback which they are able to understand, intuitively or with a little guidance. Riding promotes development of body image and balance – this is obvious to everyone. But it also promotes patience, self-control and concentration. To repeat exercises and to focus on a task teaches children openness, curiosity and

perseverance in overcoming obstacles, and also promotes the ability to learn in other areas of life.

There are many amazing stories about children and horses. A child who refused to speak outside of his family whispered "Waaalk" into an Icelandic horse's ear. When the horse started to move his "silence" was broken, and the child could speak to anyone. Changing a statement of conventional wisdom: "children need to read fairytales" into "children need to ride horses" may seem a little far-fetched considering our modern, urban lifestyles. But the miracle of children meeting horses is a gateway to a world of possibilities.

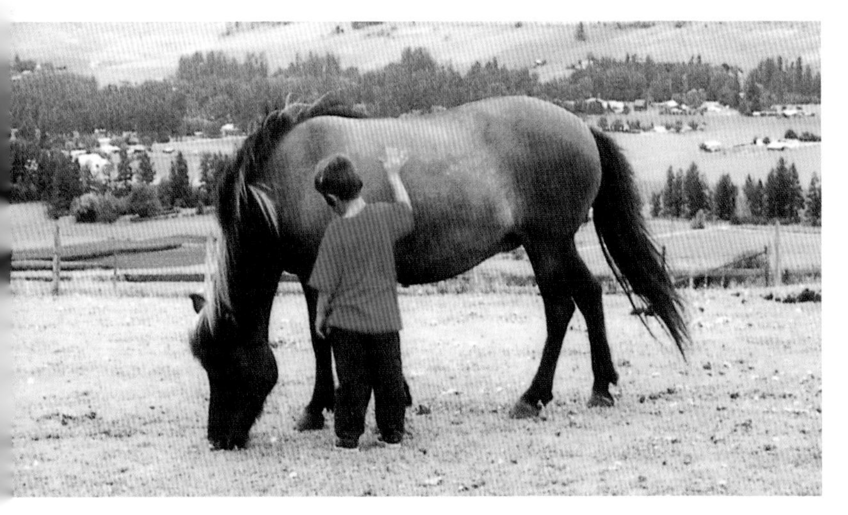

Hans Schindler is a psychologist and the head of the Institute for Family Therapy in Weilheim, Germany. He lives with his family in Bremen, and loves to ride his five-year-old Anglo-Arabian gelding, Merlin.

Small TTEAM glossary

Animal Ambassadors
Animal Ambassadors International is an educational organization dedicated to sharing the TTouch and TTEAM philosophy and techniques in order to develop a deeper understanding of animals and ourselves, and to healing our relationships with each other, nature and the environment.

Back Lifts
A TTouch that encourages the horse to contract the abdominal muscles and raise the back.

Balance rein
A seven-foot rope, one-half inch wide. It is fastened around the horse's neck and held like a second rein. It is used to slow the horse or balance him with contact on the chest combined with the normal reins attached to the bit. It has the effect of raising the horse's back and lengthening his neck. The balance rein can also be made with a twenty-one-foot long rope, one-quarter inch thick, chain stitched for a softer effect.

Balanced seat
In this seat, the rider always maintains her balance, by changing her body position through the angle of her hip joints and the stirrup length to adapt to a variety of riding disciplines.

Belly Lifts
These relax the abdominal muscles. They are useful for horses with digestive problems; provide relief for pregnant mares; help sore or stiff backs and cinchy (difficult to girth) or "cold backed" horses.

Body wrap
Elastic bandages used to wrap around the horse's body to make the connection between the forehand and the hindquarters clearer. It makes the horse feel safer. Great for both nervous and lazy horses.

Boomer's Bound
A leading position that stops the horse that is also especially helpful for head-shy horses. It prepares a young horse for mounting and loading in a trailer. The horse gets used to movements above his head from the wand being brought slowly over his neck and ears.

Chain lead line
A six-foot soft nylon lead line attached to a thirty-inch chain, which is used to do ground exercises.

Clouded Leopard
The basic TTouch. The movements are done with a slightly curved hand. The pads of the middle three fingers push the skin in a circle and the little finger follows them. The thumb makes a firm but not hard contact about two inches away from the forefinger to stabilize the fingers.

Confidence Course
This improves the horse's coordination and balance, confidence and cooperation. There are various ground obstacles made from poles, barrels, straw or hay bales, plastic, or a sheet of plywood, four feet by eight feet and one inch thick.

Cuing the Camel
A leading position to stop the horse when he has been walked forward from the Dingo exercise. The horse learns to shift his center of gravity backwards and to stop in balance from three light taps on the chest.

Dingo
A leading position that teaches the horse to engage his hindquarters and move forward from two strokes along the full length of the back and three taps on the croup. For tools we need a chain lead line and a wand.

Dolphin Flickering Through the Waves
A leading position to prepare a horse for lungeing. Also for a horse who has trouble keeping a safe distance from the handler. The horse learns to move at the desired distance from you.

Ear TTouch
A stroking or circular TTouch on the horse's ear. Working the entire ear, around the base of the ear or on the tip of the ear has beneficial effects for the horse's entire body.

Elegant Elephant
This is the strongest leading position that gives you the most control over your horse. It is especially useful for leading young horses, or for horses who have too much energy. You hold the lead line in both hands and the wand in the middle with the button end in front of the horse's nose so he can see and feel it easily.

Fanning Peacock
A leading position to keep a horse who is crowding the handler at a safe distance. You need a chain lead line and a wand.

Feldenkrais Method
This method teaches humans how to be more athletic, learn faster and use their bodies in more

effective ways. This method also helps people overcome pain and heal injuries.

Grace of the Cheetah
A leading position that encourages a horse to keep his distance from the handler and still be obedient. The handler is a little ahead of the horse and three to four feet to the side. He's able to still touch the horse with the wand by holding it by the button end.

Homing Pigeon
A leading position where the horse is led by two people who lead from opposite sides like the outspread wings of a dove. This method of leading teaches the horse to overcome his flight instinct. We use one chain lead line, a Zephyr lead and two wands as tools.

Kestrel TTouch
The way the hands are held for this TTouch gives the image of a small kestrel hawk sailing through the air with outspread wings. The hands are crossed at the wrists and both do Clouded Leopard TTouches, covering a bigger area of the horse's body. It also helps the coordination of the person doing this TTouch.

Leading positions
These are ways of leading which differ in the use of the chain lead line, the wand and the position of the handler in relation to the horse. They promote the horse's balance, coordination and cooperation and give the handler maximum influence and control of the horse.

Lick of the Cow's Tongue TTouch
A long diagonal stroke starting under the belly and going over over the horse's back.

Lindel
A bitless bridle with a stiff noseband and reins attached on the sides of the headpiece. It is also known as a sidepull and can be ordered from TTEAM.

Lying Leopard TTouch
The hand has more contact with the skin than in the Clouded Leopard TTouch and lies flatter. It allows for a warm, comforting contact on the horse's body.

Mouth TTouch
A TTouch in and around the horse's mouth, on the lips and gums.

Neck ring
An adjustable ring made of stiff rope. It is used around the neck without a bridle. It develops mutual trust and promotes a new feeling of balance of both horse and rider.

Octopus TTouch
This TTouch is done with both hands and promotes circulation and feeling in the horse's legs. It is especially useful for horses who stumble, are tense, nervous or shy.

Python TTouch
A TTouch that provides relief for tense or tight muscles everywhere. It increases circulation when done on the legs. The skin is lifted slowly with both hands and lowered slowly to the starting point.

Raccoon TTouch
A light TTouch for sensitive places. You can use it to reduce swelling. The tips of the finger pads make tiny circles with a light pressure.

Tail TTouch
Doing TTouches on and moving the tail (bending, circling and gentle pulling). "Tailwork" gives a horse a connection through the entire body, releases tight back muscles and overcomes fear of movement behind him. His self-confidence will increase.

TTEAM (Tellington-Jones Equine Awareness Method)
This method was developed by Linda Tellington-Jones and consists of bodywork (TTouches), ground exercises (Confidence Course), and riding exercises known as the Joy of Riding.

TTEAM training bit (roller bit)
The bit has a solid mouthpiece with a copper roller and a port with curved shanks. As a TTEAM training bit it is ridden with double reins.

TTouch (Tellington Touch)
A type of bodywork using circular movements and lifts to activate the horse's mind and body awareness. The TTouches are like a new language without words to deepen the bond between horse and rider. The TTouch improves a horse's health, athletic ability and teaches him to think instead of just react.

Wand
A four-foot stiff whip with a hard plastic button on the end. It is used as an extension of the arm to stroke all over the horse and give him a sense of his body. It also teaches him to respond to light signals. A white wand is preferable so the horse can see it easily and doesn't associate it with whips he's been punished with in the past. A four-foot stiff willow branch will also work.

Zephyr lead
A soft rope lead line which can replace the chain part of the regular lead on a sensitive horse or foal.

TTEAM addresses, books, videos and practitioners

TTEAM Headquarters
TTEAM and TTOUCH Training
Linda Tellington-Jones
Animal Ambassadors
International
PO Box 3793
Santa Fe, NM 87501
USA

Tel: 800-854-8326
Fax: 505-455-7233

TTEAM Secretary UK
Sunnyside House
Stratton Audley Road
Fringford
Bicester
Oxon, OX6 9ED
UK

TTEAM – Germany
c/o Bibi Degn
Hassel 4
D-57589 Pracht
Germany

TTEAM News™ International
Fleet Street Publishing
Corporation
656 Quince Orchard Road
Gaithersburg, MD 20878
USA

Books

Getting in TTouch: Understand and Influence Your Horse's Personality – Linda Tellington-Jones and Sybil Taylor, Trafalgar Square Publishing, 1995, USA.
– published in the UK under the title: *Getting in Touch With Horses*, Kenilworth Press, 1995.

The Tellington TTouch: A Breakthough Technique to Train and Care for Your Favorite Animal – Linda Tellington-Jones with Sybil Taylor, Viking Penguin Publications, 1992, USA.
– published in the UK by Cloudcraft Books, 1995.

An Introduction to the Tellington-Jones Equine Awareness Method: The TEAM Approach to Problem-Free Training – Linda Tellington Jones and Ursula Bruns, Breakthrough Publications, 1985, USA.

Videos

The TTouch of Magic for Horses
The TTouch of Magic for Cats
The TTouch of Magic for Dogs
Haltering Your Foal
Handling Mares and Stallions
Learning Exercises Part 1
Learning Exercises Part 2
Riding With Awareness
Starting a Young Horse

TTEAM instructors and practitioners

For a full list of TTEAM practitioners in your area, contact TTeam Headquarters in Santa Fe or TTEAM UK (addresses above).

USA

Trainer

Linda Tellington-Jones
PO Box 3793
Santa Fe, NM 87501

Instructors

Carol Lang
POB 3793
Santa Fe, NM 87501

Copper Love
110 South River Trail
Boerne, TX 78006

Debra Potts
18505 NE Bald Peak Rd
Newberg, OR 97132

Level 3

Jodi Frediani
1015 Smith Grade
Santa Cruz, CA 95060

Tina Hutton
POB 4363
Santa Rosa, CA 95402-4363

Ellie Jensen (Oct-Apr)
1032 C Rd
Loxahatchee, FL 33470

Ellie Jensen (May-Sep)
5418 Reeve Rd
Mazomanie, WI 53560

Patty Merrill
136 Orchard Road
Cumberland, ME 04021

Level 2

Carole Ames
Virginia Beach, VA 23456

Joyce Anderson
Rt 1 Box 31
White Post, VA 22663

Marcy Baer
RFD 1 Box 751
East Fairfield, VT 05448

Pam Beets
6181 Rosewood Dr
Littleton, CO 80121-2464

Peggy Cummings
POB 3769
Hailey, ID 83333

Judee Curcio-Wolfe
33811 SE Highway 26
Boring, OR 97009

Janice Fron
20144 Karr
Belleville, MI 48111

Marla Gibson
Box 220
Terrebone, OR 97760

Marie Hoffman
29777 Bell Rd
Kirkland, IL 60146

Priscilla Mason
19110 Pimlico
Apple Valley, CA 92308

Tom Mitchell
POB 553
Corte Madera, CA 94970

Stephanie Mosley
2199 New Franklin Church Rd
Canon, GA 30520

Wendy Murdoch
86 Summer St
New Canaan, CT 06840

Margaret Powell
5976 La Goleta Rd
Goleta, CA 93117

Marnie Reeder
7611 Old Bee Cave Rd
Austin, TX 78735

Julie Rubey
Rt 1 Box 171
Red Oak, IA 51566

Felicia Stevenson
39 Howell Rd
Laramie, WY 82070

Barbara Stender
POB 895
Summerfield, NC 27358

Dree Ward
3000 W Highway 89A
W Sedona, AZ 86336

Level 1

Betsy Adamson, DVM
20471 Portero
Redding, CA 96003

Sally Alasin
124 Scotch Pine Ct
Aiken, SC 29801

Susan Corash
409 Prospect St
Northampton, MA 01060

Lindsay Dinkins-Eden
POB 632
Ranchos de Taos, NM 87557

Dawn Hayman
3364 State Rte 12
Clinton, NY 13323

Audrey Johnson
POB 121
Campton, NH 03223

Marie Livesy
POB 175
Leggett, CA 95585

Barbara Owens
798 N Hopper Rd
Modesto, CA 95357

Jan Snodgrass
POB 173
Upperville, VA 22176

Penny Stone
26001 Budde Rd # 4302
Spring, TX 77380

Cassandra Crowley
3724 Shaunabruck NW
Canton, OH 44709

Julie Jene
N4307 Harvard Rd
Otis Orchard, WA 99027

Naomi Tyler
7756 Basin Way
Boise, ID 83703

Abby Chew Williams
RR 1 Box 1620
Monroe, ME 04951

Canada

Trainer

Robyn Hood
5435 Rochdell Road
Vernon
British Columbia
VIB 3E8

Instructor

Edie Jane Eaton
RR 1 Alcove
Quebec
J0X 1A0

Level 2

Phyllis Bauerlein
5112-114B St
Edmonton
Alberta
T6H 3N5

Olga Comeau
RR 2
Hampton
Nova Scotia
B0S 1L0

Sue Faulkner-March
136 Settlers Way
Canmore
Alberta
T1W 1E2

Barbara Janelle
169 Duchess Ave
London
Ontario
N6C 1P1

Christine Schwartz
5435 Rochdell Rd
Vernon
British Columbia
V1B 3E8

Marion Shearer
3151 Bridletowne Cr
1406 Toronto
Ontario
M1W 2T1

Jan Snowden
45 Wynford Hts Ct
612 Don Mills
Ontario
M3C 1L2

Level 1

Myles Herman
126 19533 Fraser Hwy
Surrey
British Columbia
V3S 6K7

Arlaine Holmes
1779 E 3rd Ave
Vancouver
British Columbia
V5N 1H3

UK

Level 2

Sarah Fisher
South Hill House
Radford
Bath
Avon
BA3 1QQ

Kate Prentice
Springfields
Treyford
Midhurst
West Sussex
GU29 0LD

Practitioner

Tamar Sutton
Corner Cottage
Sparsholt
Hants
SO21 2NW

Australia

Level 2

Ken and Ro Jelbart
105 Norris Rd
Pakenham
Victoria 3810

Level 1

Catherine Hamber
7 Wrench Pl
Kenthurst
NSW 2156

Practitioner

Ros Callanan
11 Brymer St
Chapel Hill
Queensland 2720

Index

Here is an alphabetical list of important names and terms that are mentioned in the book. The numbers next to them tell you on which page of the book you can find more information about that word. Page numbers in *italic* refer to illustrations.